NFT TRENDING .COM

NftTrending.com is a British Crypto Art News and Business Website

based in London, England.

NFT Trending is a collective, we used to consult global brands on crypto headquartered in central London and Silicon Valley California. Although now we would say we've found a more fulfilling role in life: coaching clients from around the world, changing lives for the better and when we're not travelling or surviving global pandemics, we try to find time to write about how success can happen.

We are in the changing lives business.

Join Our

NFT Crypto Art & Entrepenuer

Power Group

To help reinforce the learning's from our books, I strongly suggest you join our well-informed powerhouse community on Facebook.

Here, you will connect and share with other like-minded people to support your journey and help you grow.

>>>Click here to join Our Personal Growth Support Group <<<

News Site Here:

https://www.facebook.com/NFT-Trending-104426528387351

Community Group:

https://www.facebook.com/groups/nfttrending/

NFTs

NON FUNGIBLE TOKENS

By NFT Trending

Dedicated to our ever loving NFT Community at

https://www.facebook.com/groups/nfttrending/

Table of Contents

NFT Context:

The market for NFT's is huge!

- The NFT market grew by 299% in 2020!

- In their entire history $375 million worth of NFT's were sold. However, $178 million worth of NFTs were sold in just March 2021.

- The Art market alone is estimated to be worth $70 billion a year.

- Jack Dorsey's first tweet has been sold for $2.8 million!

Just a few months ago one piece of Beeple artwork sold for $6.6 million at an online art marketplace. However, recently, the digital artist sold a collection of his work through the much respected Christies auction house for nearly $70 million.

Now Hollywood agencies have dedicated an entire NFT department marking the massive growth of this new novel marketplace.

Therefore, with celebrities' rubber-stamping the approval of a new era in collectibles and agencies, entrepreneurs and marketplaces setup to facilitate the trading, it is only a matter of time before emerging NFT artists are ready and established and finally making a living off their passions.

Non-Fungible Token – Explanation:

NFTs are usually digital files such as art, audio, videos, and items in digital games; they can also be other forms of creative work.

NFT's are also known as:

- Non-fungible Tokens
- Crypto Art
- Digital Art
  And a few other variations discussed in the book.

A non-fungible token also known as an NFT for short, is a piece of data or a registered log onto a digital ledger called a blockchain. Each NFT can represent a unique digital item, and thus they are not interchangeable. This means the information to a piece of item can be stored online for all to view. This type of authentication works well with collectible forms of artwork but the potential is not limited here, it's considerable.

INTRODUCTION

The idea of digital scarcity was introduced with the advent of Cryptocurrency. Before it, reproducing any item on the internet was relatively easy. Electronic virtual scarcity has become possible thanks to blockchain technology, which is now being used to link the virtual and physical worlds. Non-fungible tokens (NFTs), also known as crypto-collectibles, are an extension of this definition. Non-fungible tokens, contrary to cryptocurrencies, are each one-of-a-kind and limited in volume.

NFTs are one of the most critical components of a modern virtual world based on blockchain technology. NFTs are being tested in various applications, including gaming, copyright, tickets, events, ID, and fine art. Furthermore, they may be able to allow for partial ownership of high-value assets. Each day, more and more of these new property kinds are generated as NFTs become easier to issue. This book will explain what NFTs are, what they can be used for, and how you can benefit significantly from their development

Ever since their introduction, NFTs have found application in so many areas

- **Artwork**

I will provide an example of how NFTs can be used to show provenance. Artwork, especially ancient artwork, is often disputed in wills. Artwork may be looted during crisis times, making it difficult to transfer the artwork to its original owner or determine its source for verification purposes.

By using an NFT to embed artwork, it gains a distinct and easily recognizable name. The fact that it is housed on the blockchain allows for a transparent and straightforward provenance method. In principle, there will no longer be any reason for prolonged legal battles over who really is the legal owner since technology could effectively resolve the problem with the proper use.

- **Sports**

When supporters watch a football game in the United Kingdom, they will get a stamp on their season ticket to show they were there. This system of verification, however, could be transformed if NFTs were introduced. With NFTs, It's easy to lend or rent a season ticket to a close friend, neighbor, or someone else who may want to go to a match whenever you can't. And when the owner does not participate, the ticket would still be verified, and the holder would be granted access for a match.

You may have the NFT connected to the person who watched the event using an NFT-type device. Football clubs could then implement a loyalty program. If you acquire all NFT for the season, you could get a prize like VIP entry or a chance to meet the football players. This isn't feasible for season ticket stamps because they're too easy to come by.

- **Music**

Be it music, movie, or other entertainment arts. Creators have failed to find mechanisms to draw audiences to their work. NFT offers a creative way to connect with potential fans by providing a digital token that can be attached to a one-of-a-kind object, such as memorabilia or one-of-a-kind events. For instance, a violin from an event tour that a guest would appreciate could be added to NFT and made available to people. Consider Zimrii's work, which has created a rewards platform to enable musicians to access things of unique value to music fans.

Likewise, NFT can be used to describe events, such as VIP entry to a show or being a member of a movie's production as an extra. NFT allows the entertainment industries to create scarcity in their production, allowing for value to be added to the scarcity and for owners to profit from their efforts.

- **Fashion**

According to recent news, Louis Vuitton introduces licenses of legitimacy for its handbags and uses blockchain to monitor items' distribution network. An NFT is essentially a mark of legitimacy. If it can be traced on a blockchain, it is unique, restricted, and to some degree, cryptographic. If the rumors are accurate, the main goal of such an endeavor is to reduce the number of counterfeit copies of the brand's iconic items.

Counterfeits will easily be detected with NFTs and blockchain platforms, and fraud can be minimized since stolen and counterfeit bags cannot be resold as the buyer will be able to verify if the seller is the original owner.

- **Investors**

The ERC-1155 standard is used in this example (more will be discussed on this standard later on in the book). It's a powerful tool to be able to issue several properties in a single contract with a combination of fungible and non-fungible tokens. In principle, this could open up possibilities that are currently unavailable in the existing financial system. Let's say you're an investor looking to invest in farmers, and you're given a list of 500 to pick from randomly.

To decide a farmer to invest in, you'd have to consider some variables, and even then, there's a lot of risks abound. Various variables can contribute to a failure, such as adverse weather resulting in low agricultural productivity. You want to put up £2,000 and earn a £200 profit. Rather than finding out which farmer would make you money, you might invest in all of them with an ERC-1155 NFT. This helps to reduce risk.

This is an intriguing use of NFTs and how the marketplace could work. In the course of reading this book, you will discover unique ways to benefit from the NFTs market.

Chapter 1:

NON FUNGBLE TOKENS

A non-fungible token (NFT) is a blockchain-based cryptographic token that denotes a single asset. These can be entirely digital assets or tokenized copies of physical assets. Since NFTs aren't identical, they may serve as evidence of legitimacy and possession in the digital world. Each unit of an asset is similar and virtually indistinguishable from one another, which is referred to as fungibility. Fiat currencies, for instance, are fungible so that individual units can be exchanged for any other equal unit. A hundred-dollar bill may be substituted for any different actual hundred-dollar bill. This is critical for an asset that is intended to be used as a means of exchange.

Fungibility is an essential feature for currencies since it allows for free trade, and there is no way to determine the past of each particular unit potentially. Nevertheless, for collectible pieces, this isn't a good quality to have. What if we might add a unique identifier to an individual unit rather than creating Bitcoin-like digital assets? As a result, each of them will be distinct from the others (i.e., non-fungible). This is basically what an NFT is.

What You Should Know

NFTs are one-of-a-kind cryptographic tokens that can't be duplicated on a blockchain. Real-world objects such as artwork, music, IDs, events, and real-estate can be represented using NFTs. Such real-world, actual assets can be "tokenized" to make them more profitable to buy, sell, and exchange while also lowering the chances of theft. NFTs may also reflect people's authenticity, copyrights, and other things.

Individual NFT's unique development allow for a variety of applications. They're a great way to digitally portray tangible assets such as real music and ticket, for instance. NFTs may also be used to eliminate middlemen and link artists with viewers or for identity management since they are built on blockchains. NFTs will eliminate intermediaries, streamline transactions, and open up a new marketplace.

Collectibles, like digital paintings, sports tickets, and copyright, account for a large portion of the current demand for NFTs. NBA Top Shot, a space to acquire non-fungible tokenized NBA experiences in the form of digital cards, is probably the most lauded place. A few of such cards have fetched vast amounts of money in auctions. Jack Dorsey, the CEO of Twitter, recently announed a link to a tokenized copy of his first tweet, in which he wrote, "just setting up my Twitter." The auction for the NFT edition of the very first tweet has already reached $2.5 million.

Understanding NFTs

Cryptocurrencies, similar to physical currency, are fungible, meaning they can be substituted or swapped for one another. A Bitcoin in the UK, for instance, is still worth the same as another Bitcoin in the US. A single unit of Ether is often equivalent to the same unit of Ether anywhere in the world. Cryptocurrencies are ideal for use as a stable means of exchange in the digital world because of their fungibility.

NFTs change the crypto model by rendering each token one-of-a-kind and irreplaceable, rendering it challenging to compare two non-fungible tokens. They are virtual representations of assets that have been compared to digital passports as every token has its own unique, non-transferable identification that allows it to be distinguished from others. They're also extensible, which means you can "breed" a third, special NFT by combining two NFTs.

NFTs, like Cryptocurrencies, have ownership information that makes it simple to identify and pass tokens among owners. In NFTs, holders may also add metadata or features related to the asset. Fair exchange tokens, for instance, can be used to depict coffee beans. Artists may also mark their digital work in the metadata with their personal signature.

Cryptokitties is probably the most well-known application of NFTs. Cryptokitties, which were first introduced in November

2017, are digital versions of cats with unique identifiers on the Ethereum blockchain. Every kitty is one-of-a-kind and has a monetary value in ether. They multiply amongst themselves, producing new youngsters with specific features and values than their parents. In the space of few weeks of their introduction, crypto kitties had amassed a fan base that had invested over $20 million in ether on buying, feeding, and caring for them. Some devotees invested over $100,000 on the project.

Although the first use case for crypto kitties may seem insignificant, subsequent ones have much more significant business consequences. For instance, NFTs have since been used in private equity and real estate investments. The capacity to supply escrow for various forms of NFTs, from events ticket to copyright, into a single financial transaction is one of the consequences of allowing several forms of tokens in a contract.

Importance of Non-Fungible Tokens

Non-fungible tokens are a step forward from the relatively straightforward definition of cryptocurrencies. Modern finance systems provide complex exchange and investment systems for a variety of asset categories, including real estate, artwork, and music. NFTs are progressing in the revival of this system because they allow digital representations of tangible assets.

To be specific, neither the concept of digital representations of tangible assets nor the application of unique identification is new. When merged with the advantages of a rigid blockchain of smart contracts, these ideas become a powerful force for reform.

Business quality is perhaps the most apparent advantage of NFTs. Converting a tangible asset to a virtual asset simplifies procedures and eliminates mediators. On a blockchain, NFTs reflect virtual or physical artwork, removing the need for representatives and allowing artists to interact directly with their fan base. They can also help businesses develop their processes. An NFT for a beer bottle, for instance, would make it easier for various players in the supply chain to communicate with it and monitor its authenticity, development, and selling during the process. Ernst & Young, a consulting company, has already created a similar solution for one of its customers.

Non-fungible tokens are equally great for managing identities. Take a look at the case of physical passports, which must be shown at any point of entry and exit. It is possible to simplify the entry and exit systems for countries by transforming each passport into NFTs, each with its own special identifying features. NFTs may also be used for identity management in the digital world, expanding on this use case.

By fractionalizing tangible assets like property investment, NFTs can equally decentralize investment. A digital property investment asset is much simpler to share among multiple holders than a tangible one. This tokenization practice does not have to be limited to real estate; it can be applied to other properties as well, including artwork. As a result, a painting does not always require a single owner. Its digital counterpart can have several owners, each of whom is responsible for a small portion of the work. Such agreements could boost the company's value and revenue.

The emergence of new opportunities and forms of investment is the most promising possibility for NFTs. Imagine a tract of land that has been divided into several parts, each with its own set of features and property types. One division might be located near a beach, while another is is a shopping center, and another is a residential neighbourhood. Each piece of land is special, valued separately, and depicted by an NFT based on its features. By integrating necessary metadata into each specific NFT, real estate trading can be streamlined, which is a complicated and cumbersome process.

Chapter 2:
HISTORY OF NFTS

Now that we know what they are, let's look at how non-fungible tokens originated.

- **Prior to the Advent of CryptoKitties**

Experiments in NFTs started when colored coins appeared on the Blockchain. Rare Pepes were among the first, with depictions of the Pepe the Frog character based on the Bitcoin counterparty scheme. A collection of Rare Pepes later sold in a live auction in New York, and some of them were sold on eBay.

- **CryptoPunks**

The first Ethereum-based NFT experiment was CryptoPunks, which composed of 10,000 notable collectible punks, each of which has a collection of unique characteristics. CryptoPunks, created by Larva Labs, featured an on-chain platform that could be used with wallets like MetaMask, reducing the limit to interaction with NFTs. CryptoPunks are definitely the best prospects for real digital antiques today, considering their small supply and strong brand within the early adopter crowd. Punks are also interoperable (more on this later) with markets and wallets since they run on the Ethereum network (though slightly less-so than newer assets, as they pre-date the ERC721 standard).

- **The Birth of CryptoKitties**

CryptoKitties was the first project to bring non-fungible tokens (NFTs) to a broader audience. CryptoKitties was a primitive on-chain game that required users to raise virtual cats together to create new cats of differing rarity. It was released in late 2017 at the ETH Waterloo hackathon. New cats may also be sold on the secondary market, and "Generation 0" cats were sold at auction in a falling-price Dutch auction.

Even though some in the gaming world later branded CryptoKitties as "not a real game," the team did a lot to innovate on-chain game mechanics given the blockchain's architecture limitations. For one thing, they created an on-chain reproduction algorithm that was concealed within a closed-source smart contract and calculated a cat's genetic code (and thus its "cattributes"). The CryptoKitties team also used a complex reward scheme to make sure of the unpredictability of the reproduction and had the forethought to reserve some low-ID cats for later use as promotional resources. Finally, they developed the Dutch auction contract, which became one of the most commonly used price discovery methods for NFTs. The CryptoKitties team's forethought gave the NFT space a big boost early on in its existence.

CryptoKitties' virality can be summed up as follows:

- **Speculative Mechanics**

CryptoKitties' breeding and trading mechanics resulted in a straight road to profit: buy a number of cats, raise them to produce a rarer pet, flip the cat, repeat (or just buy up a rare cat and expect that someone will come along and buy it). This boost the development of a breeder community, which consisted of people who were passionate about breeding and selling rare cats. Prices would grow as long as new users came in and played the games.

CryptoKitties witnessed around 5,000 ETH in volume at the peak of the trend, with Founder Cat #18 selling for 253 ETH ($110,000 at the time of sale). This deal was subsequently surpassed by Dragon's 600 ETH sale, which was valued at $170,000 at the time (September 2018), although most believe the Dragon sale was illegal. The gold rush attracted more people because of the high prices.

- **Viral Story**

The tale was also a significant part of CryptoKitties' popularity. CryptoKitties were cute, shareable, and funny, and the prospect of paying $1,000 for a virtual cat made for a great news story. Furthermore, the smart contract's overzealous users "broke Ethereum," creating a unique tale in and of itself. Higher throughput on the blockchain resulted in an increasing pending transaction stream and higher gas prices because Ethereum can only handle a small volume of transactions at a time (about 15 transactions/second). The daily figure of pending transactions increased from 1,500 to 11,000 a day. New prospective cat buyers were paying exorbitant fees and waiting for their transactions to be validated for hours on end.

The "CryptoKitty bubble" resulted from these factors: new demand entering the CryptoKitty market, prices increasing, and increasing prices attracting new demand. Of course, all bubbles will burst at some point. Average kitty prices began to fall in early December, and volume fell as well. Many people noticed that CryptoKitties' gameplay, which was rudimentary in comparison to "true games," wouldn't appeal to anyone other than speculators. The business suffered until the excitement wore off. CryptoKitties currently handles about 50 ETH per week.

- **Hype, Hot-Potato Games, And Layer 2**

Despite the market decline, many people remember the early days of CryptoKitties as a magical time. For the first time, a non-financial blockchain-based framework found its way into the world of technology, but for just a few weeks. NFTs encountered a second small hype phase in early 2018 after CryptoKitties when investors and entrepreneurs began to explore a new approach to own digital properties.

- **Layer 2 Games and Experience**

Following the release of CryptoKitties, a slew of the groundbreaking "layer two" games emerged, developed by third-party creators with no connection to the original CryptoKitties team. Creators could easily layer their own applications on top of the general CryptoKitty smart contract, which was the magic of CryptoKitties. Other than their original environment, CryptoKitties may take on a life of their own. Kitty Race, for instance, enabled users to compete for ETH by racing their CryptoKitties against one another, and KittyHats allows users to decorate their CryptoKitties with caps and paintings. Wrapped Kitties later merged Kitties and DeFi by enabling you to convert your CryptoKitties into fungible ERC20 tokens that could be exchanged on decentralized exchanges, resulting in a slew of new opportunities for the CryptoKitty market. With the creation of the KittyVerse, Dapper Labs (the newly formed company behind CryptoKitties) welcomed these ventures.

- **Hot Potatoes**

During this time, "hot potato" games became popular. You're a real NFT OG if you understand what a "hot potato" game is. CryptoCelebrities, a game, was released in January 2018. The mechanism was straightforward. Purchase a collectible celebrity NFT first. The superstar is instantly available for purchase (or "snatching") at a premium price, an increase over the original price. You make the difference between your purchase price and the new purchase price whenever anyone purchases your celebrity (minus a developer fee). You'll benefit so far if somebody is ready to purchase your celebrity. You'll be out of luck if you're trapped as the last person who holds the celebrity.

Owing to this volatile nature, the CryptoCelebrity mechanic became extremely popular, with celebrities such as Donald Trump selling for enormously high prices (123 ETH, or $137k at the time). Although the CryptoCelebrity game may have harmed the industry as a whole, we believe that experimenting with pricing and sale mechanics is an exciting part of the NFT design space.

- **Venture Capital Interest**

In early 2018, venture capital and crypto funds became interested in the NFT domain. In November, CryptoKitties earned another $15 million from large investors, taking the total earned to $12 million. Rare Bits, a blockchain game studio created by the co-founders of Farmville, earned $6 million in early 2018, as did Lucid Sight, a blockchain game studio. Forte later collaborated with Ripple to generate a $100 million blockchain gaming fund. Naspers Ventures and Galaxy Digital invested $15 million in Immutable (the business behind Gods Unchained). For a flagship Blankos Block Party game on EOS, Mystical Games earned a $19 million round headed by Javelin Venture Partners.

To further the goal of creating a broad open marketplace, OpenSea raised a small seed round and strategic investment.

- **Digital Art**

Around this time, the art community became interested in NFTs. Non-fungible tokens seemed to be a perfect match for digital art. The ability to accurately prove ownership of work and show it everywhere is a key component of what makes physical art desirable, something that has never been as valid in the virtual world. A group of enthusiastic visual artists got together and began experimenting.

Marketplaces for digital art (have also arisen. SuperRare, Known Origin, MakersPlace, and Rare Art Labs all created digital art publishing and discovery channels. Other artists, such as JOY and Josie, created their own smart contracts, establishing real brands in the room. Cent, a social network with a special micropayment framework, has grown in popularity as a place where people can share and discuss crypto art.

- **Platforms for NFT Minting**

Anyone, irrespective of whether or not they had the skills to implement a smart contract, could create an NFT using NFT minting networks.

Digital Art Chain, the first project of this kind, was introduced in mid-2018, allowing users to create NFTs from any digital image they uploaded. In the same year, a project named Marble Cards introduced an intriguing twist by enabling users to build personalized digital cards based on any URL through a method known as "marbling." This will generate a unique design and image based on the URL's content and has sparked some debate in the digital art community as a result of crypto art's "marbling."

Minting tools improved dramatically in 2019, but there was still some friction in the onboarding process. Websites like Mintbase and Mintable were created to make it simple for ordinary individuals to create their own NFTs. Influencers could easily build business cards, collectibles, and coupons using the Kred platform. Kred also collaborated with CoinDesk to develop a digital NFT "Swag Bag" for attendees at the Consensus conference. OpenSea also developed a simple storefront manager for deploying smart contracts and minting NFTs.

In 2020, these channels and Rarible and Cargo evolved to provide more functionality for bulk creation, unlockable content, and rich media. Artists, digital producers, and even musicians were able to create NFTs without needing to design a smart contract. By the end of the year, some platforms had eliminated the need to pay for the gas used in minting, rendering NFT creation completely free.

- **Traditional IP**

Traditional IP owners made many forays into the crypto collectible world after CryptoKitties. In April 2018, the MLB collaborated with Lucid Sight to introduce MLB Crypto, a mainly on-chain baseball game. F1DeltaTime was launched in collaboration with Animoca Brands and featured a $100k sale of the 1-1-1 car operated by OpenSea. In the Lucid Sight game CryptoSpaceCommanders, Star Trek debuted a series of ships, and several licensed football trading card companies, including Stryking and Sorare, went live. Panini America, one of the biggest physical collectibles stores, recently unveiled a blockchain-based trading card collectible. MotoGP is also working on a blockchain game with Animoca.

- **Expansion of Virtual worlds**

NFTs for land ownership and in-world properties have been launched in new blockchain-native digital worlds. Decentraland has launched a $10 million land sale for plots in their digital reality metaverse, following a $25 million ICO for its MANA token. For the bulk of 2018, Decentraland's LAND NFTs saw more trading volume than any other NFT. The Decentraland project is now in open beta, with certain fairly fascinating early experiences like Combat Racers, a racing game that can be played anywhere in the world.

- **NFT Crypto Headlines**

Another virtual world project, Cryptovoxels, took a more minimalist approach. CryptoVoxels began with a fundamental webVR experience in mid-2018, guided by a single developer, and has steadily extended its scope, taking care not to sell more land than is required. Today, CryptoVoxels has transacted over 1,700 ETH, and the average land price has steadily increased.

In the CryptoVoxels world, there is a gallery of digital art.

The opportunity to show off your NFTs inside the world is the most interesting aspect of CryptoVoxels (as well as Decentraland). CryptoKitty museums, cyberpunk art galleries, an NFT advent calendar, towers filled with the top NFT designs, and in-world shops where you can buy wearable pieces for your avatar have all been created by collectors. The CrypoVoxels community is constantly developing among digital artists, especially among users of Cent, a new crypto-focused content platform. Many artists are even making their own currencies, or "social money," with the help of Roll, an app that makes it simple to launch a new ERC20 token and selling their work in it.

Somnium Space and High Fidelity, a project from the developers of Second Life, are two other digital world projects that have emerged. The Sandbox recently began selling land in its Roblox-style world, which is intended to empower developers and content creators. It's one of the most eagerly awaited blockchain games to date.

Enjin extended its "multiverse" network, an environment of games based on the ERC1155 standard, after collecting 75,041 ETH in its ICO in late 2017. The ability to quickly move objects from one game to another is one of Enjin's key value propositions. The Enjin team, for instance, launched a "generic" Oindrasdain Axe (not for a particular game). This axe is now an equippable weapon in Forgotten Artifacts' game, giving players who already own it an incentive to try their game.

Trading Card Games

From the onset, trading card games seemed like a perfect match for NFTs. Magic the Gathering, a physical card game, is far more than just a game. There are hundreds of partner websites and marketplaces for purchasing, selling, and bartering. Although digital Magic games, such as Hearthstone, could potentially create an in-game marketplace for their cards, such an undertaking would be time-consuming. It would likely clash with the business model of selling new packs. Outside of the game, blockchain allows for the development of instant secondary marketplaces.

Immutable introduced Gods Unchained, perhaps the most lauded blockchain game on the marketplace currently, after a $5 million card presale. They rose to prominence after one of their professional players was suspended from Hearthstone, a digital trading card game, for participating in an on-stream political protest in Hong Kong.

For a long time prior to when the game was released, the Gods Unchained team "locked" cards (a permissible divergence from the core ERC721 functionality). Third-party marketplaces enabled users to list cards for sale during this period, although they couldn't be bought because they couldn't be exchanged. When the cards were released in November, the Gods Unchained market exploded, resulting in over $1.3 million in secondary trading value. Many other card games have slowly been gaining devoted fans. Horizon Games' Skyweaver received a $3.75 million seed round from Initialized and recently launched their public beta. Epics became the first blockchain-based collectible esports trading card CryptoSpells, a Japanese trading card game, has dominated the Japanese trading card market.

- ## **Decentralized Naming Services**

Naming services, similar to ".com" domain names though built on decentralized technology, are the third-largest NFT "asset class" (after gaming and digital art). From 2017 to 2018, the Ethereum Name Service, which was established in May 2017 and is sponsored by the Ethereum Foundation, had 170,000 ETH locked up in names (successful bids are locked up in a contract so long as the bidder holds the domain itself). The team updated the ENS smart contract to be ERC721 compliant in May of 2019, allowing names to be exchanged natively on open NFT marketplaces.

Unstoppable Domains, a venture-backed solution to decentralized naming systems, recently raised a $4 million Series A round from Draper Associates and Boost VC. Unstoppable Domains, which was founded on the Zilliqa blockchain, recently released the crypto domain as an ERC721 asset.

Chapter 3:
NFTs BUZZWORDS FOR BEGINNERS

Decentralized Exchange (DEX)

An exchange that does not require users to deposit funds until they can begin trading and does not keep their funds for them. Users instead exchange directly from their personal wallets.

Decentralized Autonomous Organization (DAO)

Decentralized Autonomous Organization is abbreviated as DAO. Basically, a Decentralized Autonomous Organization (DAO) is a set of hard-coded guidelines that describe the actions that a decentralized organization will take. Nevertheless, the word DAO may also apply to an entity known as "The DAO," which was founded in 2016 on the Ethereum blockchain.

Blockchain

A blockchain, in a nutshell, is a digital, ever-growing list of data records. A list like this is made up of numerous data blocks that are ordered in chronological order and connected and protected by cryptographic proofs.

Decentralized Finance (DeFi)

DeFi stands for "decentralized finance," and it refers to the network of financial applications designed on top of blockchain platforms. Decentralized finance (DeFi) is a trend that encourages the application of open-source software and decentralized networks to build a variety of financial services and goods. The aim is to develop and run financial DApps on a transparent and trustless foundation, such as permissionless blockchains and other peer-to-peer (P2P) protocols.

Smart Contracts

A smart contract is a form of computer software that acts as an automatic self-enforcing contract, meaning that it takes action when specific requirements are met. Smart contracts may be used as digital agreements between two entities to facilitate the transfer of cryptocurrencies (or any other digital product). The smart contract verifies that the terms of the deal have been met, and the properties are allocated accordingly.

Initial Coin Offering (ICO)

The Initial Coin Offering (ICO) is a novel method of raising funds using digital currencies (cryptocurrencies). An approach like this is more common in cryptocurrency ventures that haven't wholly built their blockchain-based product, service, or system. The funds raised at ICO events are usually obtained in

Bitcoin (BTC) or Ether (ETH), although fiat currency could also be accepted in some instances.

Bitcoin

A cryptographic-secured digital currency that is widely used as a means of exchange in a peer-to-peer (P2P) digital economic system. These frameworks are resistant to fraud and counterfeiting thanks to the use of cryptographic methods.

Nodes

The meaning of a node varies depending on the situation. In computer or telecommunication networks, nodes may serve as either a redistribution point or a communication endpoint. A node is typically made up of a physical network computer, though virtual nodes are also used.

Cryptography

In a nutshell, cryptography is the art of concealing data. Modern cryptography, in particular, employs mathematical techniques and computation to encrypt and decrypt data, as well as to ensure the security and validity of data.

Exchange

An exchange is a regulated market for trading financial instruments like cryptocurrencies, products, and securities. An exchange may be based on a physical location or a digital network. Many conventional exchanges that were once limited to physical trading are now offering digitized platforms to allow digital trading (also known as paperless trading).

Crypto wallet

In a nutshell, a crypto wallet is a platform for interacting with a blockchain network. Numerous crypto wallet forms can be classified into three categories: software, hardware, and paper wallets. They are also known as hot or cold wallets, depending on their working principle.

Altcoin

A non-Bitcoin cryptocurrency. There are thousands of altcoins, each with its own set of values and applications.

AML

Anti-money laundering (AML) is a series of rules, legislation, and protocols to stop criminals from passing off illegally acquired funds as legal earnings.

Blocks

Transactional data is stored in these files. Blocks are identical to the pages of a ledger.

Bubble

Whenever the price of a product becomes inflated, it outperforms its true value. When a bubble bursts, rates plummeted.

Decentralized

Bitcoin is a decentralized network since several different miners protect the network, as compared to a centralised network, like banking, in which body, such as the central bank, makes the decisions.

Digital Asset

A digital asset is something that is self-contained, distinctly recognisable, and has a meaning or capacity to use in binary data.

Digital Signature

A digital code that is applied to an electronically transmitted document to validate its contents and the sender's identity (generated and validated using public-key encryption).

Futures Contract

A futures contract is a contractual legal arrangement between unrelated parties to buy or sell something at a fixed price at a future date. The asset traded is typically a product or financial instrument.

Futures Exchange

A futures exchange, also known as a futures market, is a centralized financial exchange whereby individuals may trade structured futures contracts that the exchange has specified.

Github

GitHub is a web-based version-control and collaboration platform for computer programmers. It was established in 2008 and is based on Git, an open-source code management framework developed by Linus Torvalds to make software develops faster.

Gas

On the Ethereum blockchain network, the fee or pricing value is needed to perform a transaction or implement a contract effectively.

KYC

Know-your-customer (KYC) is a compliance mechanism used to check the validity of a company's customers before or around the time they begin doing business with them. Financial companies are required by law to use KYC procedures when onboarding new customers.

Mining

Miners devote computer hardware to process transactions on a blockchain (Bitcoin or other cryptocurrencies) in exchange for mining bonuses and benefits.

Mining Farm

A mining farm is a data center that is technically designed to mine Bitcoins or other cryptocurrencies. Mining farms arise due to the mining process becoming more complicated, necessitating more technological, energy, and financial resources.

Off-Chain

Off-chain transactions are those that take place on a cryptocurrency network and transfer value away from the blockchain.

On-Chain

On-chain transactions are cryptocurrency transactions that take place on the blockchain - that is, on the blockchain's records - and whose legitimacy is determined by the nature of the blockchain.

P2P

Peer-to-peer (P2P) networks are made up of computer systems that are linked to each other via the internet and allow files to be exchanged freely between them without the need for a central server.

Proof of Stake (POS)

A Proof-of-Stake system is an agreement system in which an individual's mining or validation power is proportional to the number of coins he or she owns, meaning that the more Bitcoin or altcoins a miner owns, the more mining power he or she has.

Token

In general, a token is a cryptocurrency that is not supported by its own blockchain but instead relies on another currency's blockchain features, such as ERC20 tokens, which are supported by Ethereum smart contracts.

Chapter 4: HOW NFTS WORK

NFTs are created and issued using a variety of frameworks. ERC-721, a standard for the issuance and exchange of non-fungible assets on the Ethereum blockchain, is the most well-known of these frameworks. NFTs are built on Ethereum's permanent blockchain, which means they can't be changed. No one may take away the possession of an NFT or make a duplicate of it. They're also "permissionless," which means that anyone can make, purchase, or sell an NFT without requesting permission. Finally, each NFT is one-of-a-kind and can be used by everyone.

Yes, it's like a one-of-a-kind collectible card displayed in an always-open store window that everyone can appreciate. Yet, only one individual (or cryptocurrency wallet, to be precise) may possess at any given time. A virtual artwork, such as a picture, will be basically used as a case in this book. In the NFTs platform, It's important to note, however, that it's not just about that picture (which can easily be replicated). The fact that it exists as a digital entity on the blockchain is what distinguishes it.

ERC-1155 is the latest and enhanced standard. It allows a specific contract to include both fungible and non-fungible tokens, which opens up a world of possibilities. The standardization of NFT issuance allows for greater interoperability that favors users in the long run. It essentially implies that specific assets can be easily shared among various applications. More will be explained on NFTs standardization later on in the book.

If you want to store and admire the elegance of your NFTs, Trust Wallet is the place to go. Your NFT will have an address, just like other blockchain tokens. It's worth remembering that NFTs can't be duplicated or exchanged without the owner's consent, including the NFT issuer. NFTs can be traded on open exchanges like OpenSea. These marketplaces bring buyers and sellers together, and each token has its own meaning. NFTs, by their very nature, are subject to price fluctuations in response to market supply and demand.

But how can such items be considered valuable? Like any other useful item, the value of a useful object is assigned by people who think it is valuable. Esteem is, at its heart, a common belief. You can do this in Trust Wallet with your NFTs. Your NFT will have an address, just like other blockchain tokens. It's worth remembering that NFTs can't be duplicated or exchanged without the owner's permission, including the NFT issuer.

NFTs can be exchanged on open exchanges like OpenSea. These marketplaces bring buyers and sellers together, and each token has its own meaning. NFTs, by their very nature, are subject to price fluctuations in relation to marketplace supply and demand. But how can such items be considered valuable? The value of a useful item, similar to any other valuable item, is given by individuals who know it is useful. Value is, in essence, a common belief. It makes no difference if it's fiat currency, rare stones, or a car; they all have value, and people believe they do. Why not digital collectibles? This is how any valuable object becomes precious.

Characteristics of NFTs:

Non-interoperable

CryptoPunks cannot be used as characters in the CryptoKitties game, and vice versa. This also applies to collectibles like trading cards; a Blockchain Hero card will not work in the Gods Unchained trading-card game.

Indivisible

NFTs are indivisible, unlike bitcoin satoshis, and cannot be split into smaller fractions. They only exist as a complete unit.

Indestructible

Each token cannot be lost, deleted, or reproduced since all NFT data is preserved on the blockchain through blockchain technology. The possession of these tokens is also unchangeable, implying that gamers and holders own their

NFTs rather than the companies that make them. This is in contrast to purchasing music from the iTunes store, where consumers do not necessarily own the music they are buying; instead, they are purchasing permission to listen to it.

Verifiable

Another advantage of storing past ownership data on the blockchain is that objects like digital art can be traced back to the original maker, eliminating the need for third-party authentication.

NFTs Scarcity

The maker of an NFT is in charge of determining the asset's scarcity. Consider purchasing a ticket to a football match. The maker of an NFT may choose how many replicas there are, just like an event manager can decide the number of tickets to sell. 5000 General Admission tickets, for example, are often exact replicas. A ticket with an allocated seat, for example, can be issued in multiples that are very identical yet differs slightly. In another scenario, the creator may desire to make a one-of-a-kind NFT as a unique collectible.

Each NFT will also have a specific identifier (like a bar code on a standard "ticket") and only one holder in these scenarios. The NFTs' planned scarcity is important, and it is up to the maker to decide. A maker may wish to make each NFT fully special in order to generate scarcity, or they may have good reason to make thousands of copies. Keep in mind that all of this material is available to the general public.

NFTs and Ethereum

Ethereum allows NFTs to work For a variety of purposes:

- It's easy to show ownership history because transaction records and token metadata are publicly verifiable.
- It's almost impossible to "steal" possession of a transaction after it's been verified.
- Trading NFTs can be done peer-to-peer without the need for sites that are willing to accept big commissions.
- The "backend" of all Ethereum items is the same. To put it another way, all Ethereum products can communicate with one another, making NFTs accessible through products. You can simply purchase an NFT on one asset and sell it on another. You can display your NFTs on several assets at once as a maker, and each asset will have the most recent ownership details.
- Since Ethereum is never down, your tokens will still be available to sell.

Fractional Ownership

Creators of NFTs may also create "shares" for their assets. This allows traders and fans to own a piece of an NFT without having to purchase the entire asset. This expands the number of opportunities available to NFT minters and collectors.

Fractionalised NFTs can be exchanged not only in NFT markets but even on DEXs such as Uniswap. This ensures there will be more buyers and sellers.

The price of an NFT's fractions may be used to determine its total price. You have a better chance of owning and profiting from the things you care about. It's more difficult to be priced out of buying NFTs these days. You can learn more about Fractional NFT ownership om NIFTEX, NFTX

In principle, this will allow people to do things like own a Picasso painting. You'd become a shareholder in a Picasso NFT, which means you'd be able to vote on issues like profit sharing. It's possible that having a fraction of an NFT would entitle you to participate in a decentralised autonomous organisation (DAO) for asset management in the not-too-distant future.

Ethereum-based organizations enable strangers, such as global asset owners, to collaborate safely without having to trust each other. This is because no money can be spent without the consent of the whole party. This is a developing market—NFTs, DAOs, and fractionalized tokens all progress at various rates. However, since they all speak the same language: Ethereum, all of their technology remains and can readily collaborate.

Chapter 5:
POPULARITY OF NFTS

The world of cryptocurrency evolves on a daily basis and is a real technological marvel. Since its inception as a digital medium of currency, the world has seen a boom in digital collectibles that are nothing more than one-of-a-kind virtual tokens that can reflect everything from crypto art to copyright. BNP Paribas' chief operating officer, Nadya Ivanova, discusses how these collectible digital assets can be defined as a more sophisticated version of an MP3 file.

She explains, "It enables content creators to basically own the property rights for whatever they make, enabling them to benefit from it in ways that they can't do with physical art." However, it is digital art that has acquired the most popularity. This unique identifier resides on the blockchain in the form of a non-fungible token (NFT), and just the owner of that specific NFT may possess that piece of crypto art.

Artists can display their crypto artworks in a variety of ways. It can be viewed on a computer, such as a TV or a tablet, to present it in a tangible way, or it can be done via their online profile, which includes their website, social media pages, and so on.

Artists such as Grimes and 3LAU have earned huge amounts of money from the sale of their artworks connected to these crypto tokens. Recently, Christie's New York made a splash by selling the very first NFT related to a tangible artwork: Portraits of a Mind: Block 21, by London-based artist Benjamin Gentilli, which sold for over $130,000 USD. Since then, the popularity of NFTs has skyrocketed.

Another history-making NFT work, this time strictly digital, is currently being put up for sale at Christie's for an amazing $3.25 million. In just six months and counting, the overall market share of NFTs has risen to over 350 million dollars.

Boom or Bubble

Copyright has always been a problem for content writers, particularly those who create online content. On the one hand, many social media sites immediately grant users permission to use their content. On the other hand, making a replica of the media for personal use requires simply a few mouse clicks and no producer compensation.

The NFT addresses this issue by functioning as a virtual license of authenticity, linking the actual virtual artwork to the token and giving it the same status as an artist's signature on physical work. The token can't be manipulated since it's on the blockchain and can be immediately verified by everyone on a public network.

The real original maintains its integrity due to the NFT allocated to it, allowing developers to distribute copies of their social media work openly. The ERC-1155 NFT, as previously described, is particularly beneficial as tokens for limited version sets of artwork. Internet sites such as Makerspace have sprung up as a platform for collectors and consumers, facilitating a much simpler and more open method of buying and selling digital art, similar to how financial stocks trade online. By removing the middlemen of galleries and curators, artists who have struggled to rise through the ranks of the art world elite will now exhibit their work to a much wider audience and gain a substantial income.

Nevertheless, there are fears that NFT's soaring value is an awkwardly unstable speculative bubble that could burst at any time, taking investors with it. There are also those who object to the NFTs' importance being based on artificial digital scarcity. Furthermore, the technology's recent success has resulted in hundreds of thousands of works being uploaded to its websites, preventing some from being seen by potential collectors or buyers.

Another issue is the effect of NFTs on the environment as a consequence of their strong reliance on blockchain technology.

Benjamin Gentilli, the founder of the Robert Alice Project and the artist behind the well-known Portraits of a Mind: Block 21 artwork, spoke with Analytics India Magazine about his thoughts on these issues. He acknowledged that speculation and uncertainty are "inherently corrosive to the art," however, he remains optimistic that once the considerable interest subsides, the NFT marketplace will experience a longer, more stable rise.

Kenny Schachter, a seasoned artist, writer, dealer, and collector who was one of the early users of digital art and a massive advocate of NFTs, told Analytics India Magazine that "of course, many NFTs are massively overvalued," but that overvalued assets in developed marketplace see similar speculations. This has an effect on markets generally; nevertheless, he believes that a few inflated rates should not be used to dismiss NFTs as a platform and that the present circumstance is not a bubble.

He's been working with digital art since the 1990s and claims that NFTs are the "first reliable and accurate distribution method to buy and collect such work." He went on to say that it is no more cluttered than the actual world and that while most will go unseen, demand will continue to rise in the near future.

The Growing Popularity of NFTs

Even though Bitcoin is at an all-time high, Ethereum 2.0 has just introduced its new blocks, and DeFi continues to reign supreme, NFTs are becoming more prominent in the crypto headlines.

They're even gaining celebrity support in certain situations. Ashton Kutcher, a Hollywood legend and blockchain entrepreneur, sold a piece of digital artwork via Cryptograph this summer. Pewdiepie, a well-known gamer, and YouTube personality, recently announced a partnership with Wallem, a blockchain-based game that uses NFTs for skins and other in-game properties.

Christie's, a traditionally analog auction house, announced the sale of a digital portrait of the Bitcoin code for the grand sum of $130,250, more than seven times the work's upper figure. Over 100 clubs have registered for the Sorare app, which runs a worldwide fantasy football league, including Juventus, Paris Saint-Germain, Atletico Madrid, and FC Bayern München.

Sorare enables users to create their own fantasy football teams by collecting and trading digital cards describing their favorite players. According to the aggregator website NonFungible, Sorare has risen to be one of the most popular NFT games, with over $6 million in traded volume since its introduction.

NFTs and DeFi

Despite the fact that the digital gaming market is massive and provides enormous potential for NFTs, there may be another powerful use scenario for NFTs on the horizon: DeFi. According to DeFi Pulse, the market has expanded by more than twenty times since last January. Despite their can popularity, NFTs are still relatively illiquid compared to the rest of the cryptocurrency markets, limiting their value. Now, an increasing number of projects see the benefit of combining the DeFi and NFT segments to boost both segments' value.

While this is still a very new area, one of the most important features to emerge is NFT owners' ability to stake their tokens in DeFi applications. Somebody who owns a rare Cryptokitty or a piece of Decentraland property, for example, might use their NFT as collateral for a loan, in the same manner they would ETH. NFTfi that bills itself as an "easy market for NFT collateralized loans," operates on this assumption. The borrower decides to put their NFT into a smart contract that the lender will be able to access if the borrower defaults on their payments.

This is taken a step further by Aavegotchi. Aavegotchis are pixelated collectible artworks. Each has unique characteristics that influence its overall worth and rarity in the Aavegotchi universe. Every Aavegotchi token manages an escrow contract address that holds an Aave-backed aToken, allowing Aave lending pools to generate a return. It basically means that those with Aavegotchis can use them to farm for liquidity.

The Future of NFT

Although it is clear that speculative demand drives most of the value in Non-fungible Tokens, the largest cryptocurrencies, Bitcoin and Etherium, as well as Dogecoin, both began in a similar fashion, and both have now become international platforms of trade. Since the NFT market is predominantly an instinctive market, it will benefit new investors if demand keeps growing. It isn't just artists who benefit from the technology. NFTs, according to Gentilli, is a "programmable future value development for artists," and "in the long run, I believe NFTs can help transform art, gaming, and online identity." He's not entirely wrong.

Game developers, modern "virtual real estate" sites, and even the NBA have devised ways to profit from NFTs. And now, on top of primarily open-source applications free of API constraints, cryptocurrency and blockchain developers have a whole new market to create and grow their items.

Divided Opinions

NFTs, according to their supporters, are the face of collectibles and the growing virtual resource marketplace: a way for users to prove possession of assets, whether tangible or virtual, using specific digital tokens stored on the blockchain. On the other hand, detractors have been skeptical, citing doubts about NFTs' failure to stimulate real-world scale, as opposed to crypto assets. The NFT market currently has a weekly turnover of $8.2 million. During the month of January, the weekly trading volume on bitcoin futures alone reached $500 billion.

NFTs such as digital paintings, according to critics, are simply acquired and kept instead of exchange, but as the market matures, thriving markets can arise. After all, before Musk, Saylor, and Paul Tudor Jones, cryptocurrency lacked the requisite requirement and liquidity to draw investors like them. Might the NFT landscape reflect blockchain's logical next frontier, now that the Blockchain and Ethereum protocol cryptocurrencies are well developed? Why can't you put "money" on other commodities if you can put "money" on a blockchain in the form of borderless digital assets or collateralized fiat-pegged stablecoins?

You certainly can – and many do. The million-dollar problem would be whether NFTs can produce enough interest to follow in the footsteps of bitcoin and altcoins and offer a positive return on investment, and, more significantly, whether they can provide the average investor with access to fractional investments in assets previously only available to rich collectors and high-end auction houses.

Chapter 6:
NFTs MYTH

This chapter will talk about myths since we've provided you an overview of the concept.

Demand Drives Scarcity

There was an assumption in the early days of the non-fungible token community that users wouldn't worry about NFTs' observable scarcity and would hurry to purchase them just because they were on a blockchain. Instead, we assume that demand is affected by more conventional factors such as utility and authenticity. The clear one is utility: I'll purchase an NFT ticket if it helps me to attend a meeting; I'll buy a work of art if I can view it in a digital world, and I'll purchase an object if it grants me unique skills in a game. The idea of authenticity encapsulates the tale behind an NFT. What was the source of it? Who has owned it previously? The stories of fascinating NFTs become more nuanced as the field matures, and they begin to have a meaningful effect on a token's value.

Nfts, Software-Generated Serial Number

An NFT is simply a software-generated serial number. "This token ID" belongs to "this address," according to the same software. However, there is no way to check that the token ID is connected to the virtual asset (JPG, MP4, etc.) because the token ID does not contain a hash of the virtual asset, and the digital asset does not contain a verifiable digital signature. You just have the issuer's word that they're related. NFTs are, at best, a form of "blank virtual proof" in which the blank can only be completed and assented by a third-party issuer. At the very least, NFTs would be the virtual similitude of autographs* if the creator verified them.

At least one site appears to deliver autographed digital content (tweets), but it's unclear precisely what a digital signature is or how to validate it before purchasing the NFT objectively. The "signature" tends to be an acknowledgement that in order to sell a tweet, you should connect to the cent/valuables site using your Twitter details, indicating that the operator of the Twitter account initiated the sale process. It appears to me to be unreliable, as I expected an authentic digital signature incorporated in the token that can be checked with a public key. If this flaw is verified, the cent/valuables token should resemble an "unwashed worn sweatshirt," suggesting that there is some sort of personal "connection" between the creator and the token (though it is not a digital signature).

Nfts Aren't Decentralized

People could potentially mint their own tokens and use "suitably" decentralized sale and discovery services via trusted open-source clients. Nevertheless, in the case of Nifty and other networks, that's not the case:

A third party oversees the minting operation (the "main market"). The third-party works as an agent and takes a commission. It's possible that the third party is faking it, making mistakes, or being hacked. This negates the initial advantages of using a decentralized blockchain.

The same third-party oversees the reselling mechanism (also known as the "secondary market"). In turn, peer-to-peer exchange of unique items is not possible. You'll need a centralized forum where buyers and sellers can meet and explore each other. To make buying and selling deals and connect with one another, they must first enroll on a third-party website.

The public blockchain is only used to keep track of transactions. An SQL database could store those serial numbers, transactions, and users more effectively. You can be confident that the NFT issuers' sites already store their details in SQL files, so why duplicate the details and effort?

Wrap Up

NFTs may, at best, be used to reflect virtual autographs or unwashed worn sweatshirts. Many of them are presently just "blank digital statements" with no legal validity and no connection to the actual production other than the third-party issuer's title. The use of public blockchains amounts to nothing more than a standard database with a PKI that can be accessed through APIs. The product should be offered on the creators' sites if the creator does not cryptographically verify it. They can hold auctions, create a secondary market, and provide true exclusivity. Typically, a photographer's site offers low-resolution or watermarked images, with the amazing high-resolution images being shown only after the customer has paid for them.

NFTs aren't entirely trustworthy. It all boils down to the fact that nothing that isn't indigenous to a public blockchain could be handled without risk. You fall back to conventional trust structures as soon as you bring back agents (creator, issuer, marketplace) and external assets somewhere in the system. It's entirely acceptable for artists to market their work on a third-party platform, and individuals have the right to purchase objects for demonstrative purposes. Just don't be deceived by the "trustless revolution" myth peddled by shady NFT promoters looking for a quick buck. It's fine to enlist the support of trusted third parties; there's no need to lie.

Assets with Smart Contracts

There was equally the illusion that only because a smart contract was implemented, the properties would be retained indefinitely. This ignores the fact that other organizations (websites, mobile applications) act as a gateway for daily users to connect with these apps. If these servers go down, the assets lose a large amount of value. There will definitely come a time when decentralized applications can be implemented in a massively scalable, "unstoppable" manner, but we live in a hybrid environment for the time being.

Abstracting The Chain Away

Many ventures embraced the idea of "abstracting away the blockchain" in 2018 and 2019, offering a centralized wallet with username-password protection to conceal all the functionality of NFTs from users. This was a novel approach as it enabled the same seamless onboarding as centralized applications. The issue was that the NFT environment (digital worlds, wallets, and markets) had lost interoperability. We've discovered that projects that integrate with the established NFT ecosystem, even if it means sacrificing some usability in the short term, are more appealing to the present group of early adopters.

NFTs and Copyright

The issue with how NFTs are represented is that people appear to equate them to the world of copyright, implying that the NFT grants you some kind of ownership over the visual art for which you acquired the token. In reality, this isn't the case because NFTs don't grant anyone any rights to the visual art; instead, they serve as proof that you "own" the original virtual piece. Even though you "own" the art, the final copyright owner retains control over its allocation.

Do you truly own anything with all that in your head? Both yes and no. The NFT is your receipt for the virtual artwork, but it doesn't offer you any additional rights, particularly under copyright. Only if the artist sells it to you together with the NFT, the artist retains such rights (and in most cases, they will not do so). People or corporations could theoretically claim an NFT on assets that are not their own, robbing monetary benefits from artists that don't know or care to do so. This might result in a wider distribution of works from these "authenticated" copies, which would be harmful to the artist, including the above financial loss from a missed chance to sell a legitimate NFT to your works. Artists will be able to bring copyright infringements against the sale of any NFTs (and the potential distribution of their works).

NFTs appear to be cruising the cryptocurrency craze, but one should be cautious and know what NFTs truly imply in terms of possession, as well as the consequences for copyright. While it might be great to "own" a "signed" copy of a piece of virtual artwork when you acquire an NFT, its drawbacks are just that; it's a way to show that you have ultimately acquired the genuine article, but that's it.

Chapter 7:
GROWTH OF NFTs

NFT Industry Growth and Cryptocurrency Markets

Non-fungible tokens are on the rise in terms of sports, events, ID management, music, art, investors, and everyday use. A new study analyzing 20 million NFT trades shows valuable data in several categories. However, in comparison to other cryptocurrencies, NFTs have a long way to go before receiving regular attention from major media outlets. Many conventional media outlets now monitor bitcoin rates, but big NFT transactions on OpenSea or WAX barely make the headlines.

Publicity is a significant obstacle to NFT growth. Unlike crypto assets, which are traded publicly, NFTs are traded privately. One marketplace is open to the public, to put it another way, while the other is concealed in the shadows. However, NFT aggregator platforms, such as NonFungible.Com, provide much-needed transparency to trading activity. However, cryptocurrencies, and the blockchain technology that underpins them, ironically paved the way for NFT growth and use cases. NFTs have the ability to raise much faster than cryptocurrencies for a variety of reasons.

Let's take a look at three of them.

- Affordability

In theory, the definition of meaning is a little hazy. Since other individuals think something is necessary, we believe it is. Why is it that government-issued money has little value? That's why, according to the system.

Money is an odd creature. Money is, besides, just a promise encased in common metals, plentiful (and renewable) paper, and splashing of ink! Finances are a challenge for most people on a macro, and sometimes a budgetary, stage. The same can be said for cryptocurrencies. If individuals have difficulty understanding money, digitizing it just adds to the confusion.

But what about tokens? The idea of buying an item with a particular and specific use case is something that most individuals can understand. Anybody who has ever visited an arena to play video games would understand. This takes us to our next step.

- Gamification

Cash, let's face it, is dull. Yes, some of the extravagances and experiences that money can purchase can be thrilling. However, looking at numbers in a spreadsheet isn't really our idea of a good time. NFTs, on the contrary, are often associated with gameplay and artwork. In addition, their scarcity and collectability are helping to increase NFT consciousness. NFTs cater to musicians, enthusiasts, players, and combinations of all three for a number of reasons.

NFTs offers gamers the ability to claim ownership of their in-game pieces. OpenSea is the biggest NFT market in the world. However, as the public's understanding of NFT increases, more are springing up, including Nifty Gateway, which a billionaire owns. Nevertheless, since OpenSea is the most well-known of the group, we find the most observable data there.

From a handful in mid-2018, the number of OpenSea users has recently exceeded 19,000. Although the figure is small, the upward trend is remarkable. NFTs and blockchain games go hand in hand. NFTs are riding the surge in tandem with video games, which are on a nearly never-ending increase in popularity.

- Deeper Foundation

You would be able to connect if you were alive before the Great Crypto Bullrun of 2017. For almost a decade, cryptocurrencies have been flying under the radar. When bitcoin's value soared past $20k per coin, however, the whole world appeared to take note. You may or may not have a Coinbase account, but regardless, it is one of the most fluid fiat-enabled exchanges in the world. You can possibly guess what this massive rise in crypto wallets means for the NFT industry. The adage "a rising tide raises all boats" is probably familiar to you.

Since NFTs and blockchain games often connect to crypto wallets, 30 million users provide a great starting point. And that number is based on a single transaction. Hundreds of trades and wallet apps now give NFTs a home, both now and in the future. Instead of starting fresh, NFTs have a firm base on which to create layers. The increasing growth trend of non-fungible tokens can be traced back to the creation of bitcoin and ethereum.

- NFT Use Case

It's not simply a piece of art. Recently, Jehan Chu, the owner of blockchain investment firm Kenetic, paid $84,000 for 680,000 Handshake (HNS) NFTs, which offer the bearer the power to issue. The Handshake blockchain is used to extend NFT website domain extensions. NFTs, according to Chu, is the "real missing link between online and offline items," and he believes they have the potential to transform industry, economy, society, and history. To say that this is a bold assertion is an understatement.

NFTs gain from transparency due to their documentation on a public ledger, which adds a layer of security to collectible property that individuals tend to be attracted to. NFTs have been rumored to play a vital role in the decentralized finance (deFi) market, and there has been proof of concept in the form of Alpaca City's Ethereum-based digital world. The pre-sale of Alpaca's November tokens sold out in under 20 minutes, earning nearly 1,000 ETH. Alpaca NFTs will not only be "bred" (remember CryptoKitties?) by their owners. Boosting the value of tokens, such as NFT-collateralized loans, interest-bearing accounts, and so on, could be the NFT industry player. NFT owners would like to send and receive assets from different blockchains, so compatibility will be crucial.

DeFi primitives are presently available on well-known blockchains such as Ethereum and TRON. TRC-721, the latter's own NFT standard, has now been announced, allowing users to track and pass tokens on the high-throughput platform. NFTs are being considered significant by individuals on both sides of the argument. Firm s are providing safe and open NFT protocols, while buyers are anxious to get skin in the game. A network of smart contracts Hashmasks, CryptoPunks, and Decentraland are only a few of the NFT projects on Ethereum.

Why You Should Invest in NFTs

Because of the following reasons, NFTs have proved to be a worthwhile venture:

- Creates Value for the Tokenized Asset

NFTs provide a means by which tangible items such as artworks can be tokenized, preventing replication and giving exclusive ownership to the creator. This, in essence, generates scarcity and, as a result, demand for the artwork.

- It Increases Liquidity for Investors

Tokenizing assets helps investors to have better leverage on their assets whenever they need it. A digital property owner, for instance, may choose to rent out his or her digital property to advertisers or marketers for a price while still owning the property. In this situation, the digital property actually belongs to the owner, but a portion of it has been liquified as rent.

- Growth and development opportunities

NFTs have the potential to expand and improve the land market. For example, in real estate, owning and managing virtual lands provides the ability to determine what you like to do with your property, and tying NFTs to land pieces has shown tremendous room to grow and develop. You have the option of renting it out, creating a stable and robust business for advertising, or selling it online.

NFT Projects with Increasing Growth

- **Art Tokens**

Boyart OpenSea store has auctioned artworks valued at over 400 ETH, with newer products fetching prices of over 75ETH. Boyart is a skilled artist who has previously sold a few of his arts in tokenized form. The new mural paintings are wrapped in freshly minted NFTs and auctioned off.

Boyart has demonstrated that the crypto space can effectively create an art marketplace in a matter of months, attracting investors to acquire assets of interest. Boyart's murals can also be found in the Digital Museum of Crypto Art.

- **Lil Moon Rockets**

Lil Moon Rockets is a new NFT project that uses smart contracts to distribute one-of-a-kind works of art. The project incorporates vector art and computational genealogy to keep up with current trends. So every user will get their own Moon Rocket image just after the original offering of artwork. Lil Moon Rockets is using a special "blind sale" method to prevent project investors and initial users from buying up the most useful art. All artworks will be announced at the end of the smart contract. Unlike many NFT projects based on the Ethereum blockchain, Lil Moon Rockets uses the Binance Chain to issue its NFTs and subsequent "name your rocket" tokens. While NFTs have been valuable to Ethereum's revenue, Binance Chain allows for easier transactions with lower fees.

- **Cryptopunks**

When it relates to NFTs, crypto punks are among the most standardized art forms. Their popularity exemplifies the attraction of NFTs. Cryptopunks skyrocket, becoming one of the most popular collections despite the standardized art.

Cryptopunks became a go-to for risky investments and collections after specific social media marketing from influential crypto personalities. As a result of a combination of scarcity and increasing popularity, the 10,000 Punks characters are equally enjoying a stable resale market. Those NFTs began modestly enough, with a free airdrop to anyone with an Ethereum wallet who wishes to acquire one, with prices approaching $57,000. The price has no limit, regardless of how the early tokens were allocated because network effects of popularity created the highly active market.

- **Beeple's artwork**

On the NFT global market, an artist referred to as Beeple, that had been active on Instagram for years, and yet just recently attained recognition. Beeple's work is highly regarded, with comparisons to Pascal Boyart. However, the more computational approach, which combines art and technology, is also valued by the market.

- **Hashmasks**

One of the most notable projects in the NFT space is Hashmasks. The collectibles are designed in a postmodern style, with alien or robotic figures and backgrounds. Artists' work, as well as computational combinations, were used to piece together over 16,000 images. In crypto-related social media, hashmasks are becoming an identity mark. It's impossible to say where the works of art will end up. They've been used as visual identities and in social media games up until now. Only weeks after its initial launch, the most costly hashmask has already attained a price of 420 ETH, with others costing between 2-4 ETH.

Chapter 8:
NFTS MARKET

Market Expansion

Following the CryptoKitties boom in late 2018, the number of unique accounts communicating with NFTs has gradually increased, from 8,500 in February 2018 to over 20,000 in December 2019. A small number of influential users appears to be driving the market. The median seller on OpenSea has traded $71.96 worth of items, while the average seller has traded $1,178 value of things, showing that there are a lot of power sellers. It's worth noting that large accounts, such as official game accounts, raise the average. The average OpenSea buyer spent $943.81 on their purchases, while the median buyer paid $42.72.

Provided the market's age, the best way to gauge its progress is to focus on a major driver: investor interest in the region. As new investors join the room, the number of mainnet ERC721 contracts has risen exponentially over the last year, reaching the 1,000s in June of 2019.

Mechanisms of Sale

On decentralized markets, NFTs are presently sold mainly for ETH. Interestingly little trade occurs in stablecoins such as DAI or USDC, owing to the difficulty in obtaining stablecoins. Lower-ticket products are usually sold through Dutch sales and fixed-price sales, whereas larger-ticket items, such as super-valuable Gods Unchained cards or classic game items, are generally sold through English (eBay-style) sales. Bundles are also a common way to sell, with the percentage of package sales rising steadily.

NFT Distribution

One would wonder how much overlap there is between different NFT ventures. Is there a lot of bleed-over between groups around projects (Gods Unchained players only play Gods Unchained), or are they still isolated? Is it possible for a CryptoKitties fan to also own an ENS domain and engage in the virtual art ecosystem?

NFTs Marketplace

The top NFT markets cater to a growing community of NFT owners, fans, and investors interested in one of the most thrilling asset classes to emerge in recent years. Some markets are just for unique dapps, so they're at the bottom of the list.

Let's take a look at the most common NFT marketplaces:

- **OpenSea**

The first and largest peer-to-peer NFT marketplace for crypto products is OpenSea. You may think of it as a blockchain-based eBay. Collectibles, game pieces, and other virtual products protected by a blockchain are among the items accessible.

Such products can be bought, sold, or traded with anyone worldwide on OpenSea. OpenSea is the biggest world marketplace for user-owned virtual assets, with over 4 million products and the most diverse collection of categories.

- **Rarible**

Rarible is a modern technology (NFT) marketplace similar to OpenSea. It also serves as a forum for the development of NFTs. Users may generate an NFT using content they own, including a digital picture or motion graphic, by going to Rarible. Sellers can make many NFTs for a single image and sell it several times. Alternatively, distribute only one object, which will be considered rarer. Additionally, artists may specify a percentage of lifetime resales that they choose to earn.

NFTs may be purchased in order to create a portfolio. Some are creating personal portfolios of what they want, while others are amassing a collection of art that they believe will hold value in the future.

- **SuperRare**

SuperRare is a social forum that promotes crypto art production and selection. SuperRare was founded by John Crain, the CEO of Pixura, and Jonathan Perkins, the company's

Chief Product Officer. Ever since its inception, SuperRare has collaborated with artists and points to cater to artists' and buyers' concerns.

SuperRare may be considered the high-end version of Rarible. The entry requirements are more stringent, and artists must apply their work for acceptance before being identified. On the other hand, everyone can participate on rarible.

- **Atomic Assets**

Atomic Assets is a portion of the Atomic Hub dedicated to market listings for WAX-hosted NFTs. Street Fighter, Cogs, and Blockchain Heroes are examples of NFTs. Users must register for a WAX cloud account or sign in with Anchor or Scatter to make use of the marketplace, which has a familiar interface. The WAX blockchain has held a strong claim on the NFT market, having actually completed several sold-out promotions in collaboration with labels such as Topps, Blockchain Heroes, and Street Fighter during 2020.

- **Known Origins**

Artists and designers may use Known Origin to build, find, and own rare digital artwork, all while being protected by the Ethereum blockchain. The KnownOrigin gallery accepts digital artwork in the form of jpg or GIF files. IPFS serves as a decentralized storage system for all files. All properties are assigned special, trackable identifiers.

Known Origin focuses on digital art, so looking for Cryptopunks or Avastars, for instance, is pointless. Consider the pieces for sale here to be similar to those found in an art gallery.

- **Axie Marketplace**

Axie Infinity is a Pokemon-inspired digital pet universe in which players use their adorable Axies in various games. The Axie Infinity Universe uses a "Play to Earn" gameplay system and a player-owned ecosystem to demonstrate blockchain technology's advantages. Players will carry their Axies to the market and sell them in an auction format.

Depending on the seller's purpose, the price will rise or fall from the starting price to the final price over time. Other players must be well-organized in order to take advantage of the opportunity to purchase desired Axies from sellers. Axie Marketplace is a great place to start.

- **Decentraland Marketplace**

The Ethereum blockchain powers Decentraland, a decentralized digital reality network. Users will make, discover, and monetize what they develop and own in the Decentraland environment. Users can purchase property, regarded as "parcels," in the decentralized digital environment registered on a blockchain-backed ledger. The land is a form of non-fungible virtual product or service token called LAND, held in an Ethereum smart contract, as are the virtual assets constructed on top of it.

Owners of land have power over the material published on their property, which is coded into a smart contract. Scenes and photographs, as well as games and software, may be included in this material. Users can fly, discover, and visit places in the same way they would in the actual world. Users can communicate on the platform via a peer-to-peer network.

- **Viv3**

VIV3 is the Flow blockchain's initial broad market, based on the premise that the globe is on the verge of transitioning from physical to virtual property. By leveraging Flow, Viv3 hopes to inspire a million individuals to make, exchange, and own the world's most expensive assets. A flexible and composable smart contract framework that provides the performance needed for mainstream applications.

VIV3 is used by artists, game studios, and brands to create one-of-a-kind tokens that reflect their digital works on the Flow blockchain as NFTs (Non-Fungible Tokens). Fans, owners, players, and virtual asset investors buy these NFTs.

- **TreasureLand**

TreasureLand is the Binance Smart Chain's first and biggest NFT platform, allowing users to buy and sell BSC NFT tokens. It's a spinoff from the creators of DEGO, a hybrid platform that combines DeFi and NFT technology. NFT Casting, Mining, Crafting, Auction, Trading, and more are all part of the ecosystem.

On the Treasureland market, getting hold of some NFTs is a breeze. It helps for listings and auctions to be paid in a variety of cryptos. You may also move to DEGO to participate in NFT mining, which is unusual in the collectibles environment.

- **NFT Showroom**

NFT Showroom is a blockchain-based virtual art platform powered by Hive, a quick and reliable blockchain. Artists may sign up for their virtual works and offer rare tokens that can be exchanged on the platform as "evidence of art." The Hive group has been buzzing about the NFT Showroom, and it's one to keep an eye on because of its pace and low cost.

- **Arkane Market**

Arkane Market is a virtual collectibles platform for gamers and overall owners that do not accept cryptocurrency payments. Arkane Market is equally the first non-financial transaction (NFT) platform to run on Polygon (Formally Matic). Even though the marketplace is still in its infancy, it recently opened with a Battle Racers initiative to generate instant interest.

- **Ghost Market**

The first-ever cross-chain NFT Market is the Ghost Market. It lets you search for, purchase, and auction NFTs on the NEO and Phantasma Blockchains. Phantasma is a swift, stable, and flexible blockchain explicitly designed for NFTs, so it comes pre-loaded with various NFT features (minting, batch minting, sending, and so on).

Chapter 9:
HOW TO MAKE MONEY WITH NFTs

An Investment Opportunity

We are, without a doubt, an unusual species. There are several billion-dollar industries around collectibles and art over the centuries. Millions of individuals are engaged in the production of these products. Mega-cap companies such as Sotheby's and Christie's and online entities such as eBay and Etsy now assist in transacting and profiting from collections. Individuals spend a small fortune on insurance to protect themselves from fraud and injury. And those in the know can amass considerable wealth.

A similar principle is applied to NFTs. Although digital art is easier to copy and distribute, several individuals still want to own the original. Many people are motivated by a mixture of love and pride; Brunei's Sultan is said to have 7,000 cars in his collection. Others, on the other hand, want to thank the actual creator for making something they like. Thousands of independent virtual artists sell their art for less than $100 on Etsy. And if you want a specific artist, I highly urge you to purchase an inexpensive piece or two, even if it's only to help the creators keep doing what they're doing.

If you're in it for the money, however, you're possibly just asking for one thing. Are non-financial-transactions (NFTs) a good investment?

Here's the secret: NFTs are just as strong as the asset they're based on.

The $590,000 selling of the popular Nyan Cat Gif, for example, could only have happened because of the meme's enormous success over the years. Likewise, the NBA's top-selling NFT was a highlight reel of LeBron James, that went for $200,000. On the other hand, less well-known players had reels that went for as little as $9.

To put it another way, in order to benefit from NFTs, investors must have a unique understanding of the assets they represent. Basketball fans who can accurately predict potential NBA star players can acquire cheap highlight reels now and make millions by the time the stars break out in a few years. Both Steve Nash and Kobe Bryant had poor newbie years (Kobe averaged just 7.6 points per game at the age of 18!) but went on to become huge stars in later years. And any team that bet on them earlier might have significantly profited. Those who purchase NBA one-hit sensations as NFTs in their 20 minutes of fame, on the other hand, would not do as well.

Likewise, there have always been stars and duds in the world of art. Banksy, a famous street artist, had several of his early works painted over by officials who misidentified them for graffiti. Meanwhile, his later works at the sale will fetch as much as Rembrandt's. Ordinary people also have trouble distinguishing between masterworks and average works of art. To put it another way, if you wish to earn a lot of money in NFTs, concentrate on your field of expertise. If you enjoy video games, check out Decentraland. The NBA's NFTs might be for you if you're a sports fan with a keen eye for talent. And if you're terrific at art or music, make that your area of specialization. For decades, the same idea has been applied to stocks.

Ideas for NFTs

NFTs do not have to be works of art, copyright, ID, or event. It may as well be useful in and of itself. Take a look at some other NFT-making ideas in addition to those described earlier:

- Flight Tickets
- Support token for influencers
- Coupons for supermarket discounts
- Static or animated 2D images
- Images in three dimensions
- Things related to video games
- Videos
- Articles for the blog

Term definitions

- ## Ethereum

Ethereum is a blockchain, and ETH is the currency used to render Ethereum blockchain transactions.

- ## Gas Fees

Consider gas fees to be the costs of Ethereum blockchain transactions. Gas prices are dictated by supply and demand across the system, not by the blockchain.

- ## Crypto wallet

A cryptocurrency wallet is a software or hardware interface that enables users to store and recover virtual assets.

- ## Wallet address

Your wallet address is a one-of-a-kind address. Whenever people send crypto or NFTs to your crypto wallet, they will use this address.

- ## Seed Phrase

If you forget your password or lose access to your wallet, your seed phrase is a list of terms that can be used to retrieve your crypto. Discover your seed phrase and save it anywhere secure, preferably in different locations, when you first start trading with your wallet. Do not share your seed phrase with someone or save it on a digital cloud storage platform.

- **Collection**

A collection is a body of art, similar to a shop or gallery. Don't be puzzled. For example, if you hear anyone refer to an OpenSea collection as a store or gallery, they're the same thing. To keep it clear, we call it a collection.

User safety

Cryptocurrencies and blockchains have some advantages, but you should do your homework on how to store funds and digital objects before diving in securely. You are solely responsible for the crypto and NFTs in your wallet. Never give out your seed phrase or password to someone.

Setting up your wallet

To begin, you'll require a wallet to hold your cryptocurrency and NFTs. I suggest downloading the MetaMask wallet extension on Google Chrome. For your convenience, here are the MetaMask FAQs! After that, go to a marketplace, for example, OpenSea, and then set up your Profile. Follow the directions in your wallet after Signing In.

Creating your collection

You can now see your account page – it's currently empty, but it probably in progress! We're not creating NFTs at this moment; we're just going to set up your collection so you can show off your work, and you can change all of this later.

Purchasing Ethereum (ETH)

Find a trustworthy and controlled seller in your area on the internet and buy marginally more ETH than the price quoted when you click "Post Your Listing." Due to network congestion, the gas fee needed to set yourself up for trading varies between $50 and $250 and varies with marketplaces. Stay updated on the figures on your page if you want to keep a record of how rates are shifting and wait for a drop. Return to the marketplace and wait for your new balance to appear in your wallet. Once the funds have been issued, you can begin the listing process.

How to Create NFT

First and foremost, settle on a token standard. It's essentially a set of rules that describes a token. There are currently two widely used token standards: ERC721 and ERC1155. ERC721 is an Ethereum blockchain token standard. The Enjin blockchain uses the ERC1155 token standard. Since it has a class property, ERC1155 is more complicated. A baseball card, for instance, is a category if you have many digital baseball cards. You may decide how many cards you like to submit or obtain in this way.

Next, decide what type of NFT media you would like to create. It could be 2D or 3D art, a static or animated design, or a player-interactive object. Ensure this file is hosted on a public URL and that the file name ends with the correct extension. Minting NFT is the technical term for creating NFT. Let's look at how to build an ERC721 NFT:

Load an Ethereum wallet on your browser. For instance, Chrome or Firefox with the Metamask extension or the Brave browser. To build an ERC721 smart contract, download the Mintable app. Mintable requires you to link your Ethereum wallet. Create your own smart contract. The contract's name should reflect the type of assets you intend to produce.

Give your contract a name. GME, BTC, ETH, TSLA are examples of stock and cryptocurrency tickers. It is possible to mine in batches. It enables you to create multiple NFTs at once. Fill in the web address where your file can be found. Up to three rows of metadata may be filled in. These are the attributes of your token. Color: Red, Size: Big, Shape: Circle, for instance, could be the property of your token.

Whether or not to use Mintable's API is up to you. You'll be able to add more custom metadata properties as a result of this. It also allows you to sell your NFT on the OpenSea marketplace quickly. Name, groups, and definition are only a few of the properties that can be filled in.

There are two charges to pay. The expense of making a smart contract is one charge. Since Metamask uses a smart contract on the blockchain, the gas fee is large. The limit is set at 3,500,000 gwei. If you change something, the payment will fail. The second payment is for the transaction's handling. You can simply set this to a minimum of 1 gwei, but processing will take 1-2 hours. A smart contract will be produced once you authorize the creation.

How to Buy NFTs

Nifty Gateway, MakersPlace, SuperRare, OpenSea, Decentraland, and Rarible are only a few of the many markets where you can buy NFTs.

How to sell NFTs

What is the safest way to sell NFT?

NFTs, like every other marketplace, have their own trading areas. Pay attention to which a marketplace supports token standard. You'll need to sign up for an account and connect your cryptocurrency wallet. For example, If you've created NFT on Mintable, you can sell it on OpenSea with ease.

Here are several more websites where you can sell your NFT:

- Nifty Gateway
- Rarible
- Terra Virtua
- OpenSea
- Async
- MakersPlace
- SuperRare
- KnownOrigin
- Mintbase
- Mintable

Good luck with creating and selling your NFTs

Chapter 10:
FUTURE OF NFTs TECHNOLOGY AND ASSET

The current business world is monopolistic. Decentralized transactions allowed by NFT may be a viable option that saves small businesses and social entrepreneurs. Almost every year over the last five years, the blockchain environment has added to its list of disrupted industries. The now-famous initial coin offering (ICO) boom occurred in 2017 and 2018. Smart contracts took over the spotlight the next year.

Paving the Way For Creativity

By implementing smart contract functionality and thus giving birth to flexible technology platforms, Ethereum (ETH) developed into a major actor in the scene (dApps). This made it possible for everyone to build their own dApp, obviating the need for traditional tech behemoths.

Decentralized finance (DeFi) effectively decentralized most, if not all, conventional financial firms' operations in 2020. It allows users to engage in a wide range of peer-to-peer transactions, including lending and investing, staking, yield farming and even betting. Moreover, the DeFi recent surge created a new decentralized financial model and opened the way for future developments.

Non-Fungibility and New Possibilities

Using the prior years' advancements, the non-fungible tokens (NFT) technology appears to be advanced enough to witness a surge of its own in 2021.

The principle of non-fungibility leads to new types of transactions, in which consumers are not restricted to monetary transfers but may also enjoy asset exchanges, whether digital or physical.

The transacting entities' transaction details are also saved, and the asset's royalties are permanently recorded on the smart contract. To put it another way, NFTs are poised to control the next wave of trade, namely decentralized commerce (or dCommerce).

Given the presence of the ERC-721 protocol just a couple of years ago, the question "why haven't NFTs and dCommerce been the next big thing?" is a fair one. It is a basic framework for non-fungible tokens, also known as deeds, in simple terms. Nevertheless, it is crucial first to comprehend the system through which they function and the scheme that they appear to be undermining.

Tech Firms Becoming E-Commerce Oligarchs

Even though e-commerce revolutionized the conventional physical commerce status quo, it abused the idea of online peer-to-peer (P2P) commercial transactions for its own benefit. A few tech firms rapidly rose to e-commerce oligarchs' status, running large swaths of global commerce. For example, in 2020, Amazon's sales volume make up about half of the US e-commerce retail market. Such monopolies have been abusing their position as intermediaries for more than 20 years by accumulating customer data and harvesting the surplus value generated by users.

The data-protection trend of recent years has expanded into data-management activities in various sectors, including e-commerce.

Various blockchain-based initiatives have tried to challenge the conventional e-commerce system by providing alternatives to existing data storage and transaction procedures, empowering consumers.

Regardless of the fact that such first-layer dCommerce interventions have laid the groundwork for freeing consumers from monopolistic behemoths, specific customer needs (such as trust, decentralization, and data transparency) remain unmet. As a result, the time is not yet ripe for widespread acceptance of such services.

Powering the Next Generation of E-Commerce

The NFT technology will now benefit from its crypto predecessors' hard work and fuel the next decentralized commerce wave. Consumers will benefit from a new age of peer-to-peer exchange by using NFTs to replace e-commerce intermediaries. This groundbreaking innovation, which NFTs will allow, will return control to the customer.

It will also encourage smaller retailers to regain their foothold in the face of e-commerce behemoths' rising control, decentralizing, and demonopolizing commerce. What is a more worthwhile endeavor for crypto pioneers than that? The crypto world's present economic operation is restricted to virtual products only, isolating the multi-trillion-dollar actual-world commerce sector from smart contracts and the next-generation network. It could be debated that the surge of NFTs should be enough to spark a radical shift in this area. The economy of things must not be restricted by its "digitality": digital assets and services ought to be mixed with physical goods.

It's Time For Action

The technology is already in place; it is down to our industry's crypto influencers to take action. NFTs have the technological framework to eliminate the need for human intermediaries and allow for the redemption of physical assets in a completely new way. The effort to exchange "stuff" that can vary from baseball cards to BMWs to homes, as NFTs can then be tokenized and standardized from digital to physical redemption

On the one hand, it is undeniable that e-commerce behemoths have routinely exploited consumers and their dataflows, increasing complexity and prices in the digital product trading phase.

Furthermore, the DeFi scene has shown how important it is to disrupt existing monopolizing systems, even though it appears to be a difficult task at first. When you consider that using NFTs to drive trade would give small retailers a fair shot while also allowing customers more access to the products they want, realizing this target appears to be a primary concern.

Nonetheless, the NFT technology has evolved enough to act as the foundation of a new commerce age, where everyone can trust and use a genuinely peer-to-peer commerce platform free of third-party mediators and arbitration fees.

Ethereum and Future Prospect For Nfts

Those of you who are interested in learning more about cryptocurrency have already heard the basics. Though Bitcoin is the most widely used cryptocurrency in this field, I want to draw your attention to the value of Ethereum, mainly how it facilitates the growth and development of NFTs. If you've heard of it or not, this blockchain has proved to play an essential role in defining today's crypto marketplace and is a name you should be familiar with.

Why You Should Care

NFTs also uncovered a creative side of crypto that is exciting to play and understandable, and open to newcomers. When more well-known figures host their first NFT, they attract a new wave of interest from their millions of followers who are learning about crypto for the first time. Individuals are in a unique position to curate and explore this burgeoning wave of scarce digital content as a result of this. Showtime combines NFTs to create an Instagram-like interface, and Catalog, a new music-focused NFT platform, is launching a digital record store.

As Nifty Gateway drops keep selling out in seconds thanks to credit card purchases and unrestricted transactions, new collectors are discovering new methods to collect their favorite artists and items. This phenomenon will only develop in the near future.

NFTs Bubble

What's going on in the NFT ecosystem right now is nothing short of a radical change for the cryptocurrency industry as a whole. There's no doubt that the vast majority of consumers are here to guess, as ardent collectors frame their virtual artwork using companies like Infinite Artifacts. This rapid growth indicates interest, but it is eerily similar to the 2017 ICO boom, which led to a market collapse several years ago.

Nevertheless, a large wave of foundational companies and products, such as Uniswap and Compound, emerged from that multi-year bear market. The same is likely to happen with NFTs. Until then, keep in mind that virtual content has value, and crypto enthusiasts are lining up to get their names etched on tomorrow's most valuable collections.

Chapter 11:
NFTs STANDARD

Standardization

Conventional virtual properties, such as event tickets and domain names, lack a single virtual representation. A game's in-game collectibles are possibly represented differently than an event ticketing scheme. Creators may create universal, interchangeable, inheritable standards for all non-fungible tokens by defining them on general blockchains. Basic primitives such as possession, sale, and easy access control are included. Different standards (for instance, criteria for displaying an NFT) can be layered on top for more decadent display within applications.

These are similar to other virtual essential components such as the JPEG or PNG image file format, HTTP for inter-computer requests, and HTML / CSS for web content presentation. On top of that, blockchains add a layer that provides creators with a whole new collection of stateful primitives to construct applications on.

Interoperability

Non-fungible token standards make it possible for non-fungible tokens to travel freely between environments. Whenever a creator releases a new NFT project, the NFTs are instantly accessible in hundreds of wallet providers, exchangeable on markets, and, more lately, displayable within digital worlds. This is possible since open standards include a simple, reliable, dependable, and permissioned API for reading and writing data.

Tradeability

Free exchange on digital markets is the most persuasive aspect allowed by interoperability. For the first time, holders can transfer products out of their existing ecosystems and into a market in which they can leverage advanced trading features, including eBay-style sales, bidding, merging, and the capacity to sell in any currency, like stablecoins and application-specific currencies. Tradeability of products reflects a shift from a capitalist economy to an open, free-market economy for game developers. From resource availability to marketing to capital management, game developers no longer have to handle any aspect of their economy. Instead, they should delegate the heavy lifting to free markets!

Liquidity

Non-fungible tokens with fast tradeability would have more liquidity. NFT markets will appeal to a wide, wide range of people, from experienced traders to newcomers, allowing products to be exposed to a larger pool of buyers. NFTs widen the demand for specific virtual products in a similar way that the 2017 ICO explosion gave birth to a new product class powered by rapidly liquid tokens.

Immutability and Provable Scarcity

Creators may use smart contracts to set strict limits on non-fungible tokens' availability and impose permanent assets that cannot be altered once the tokens are released. For instance, a creator can algorithmically limit the number of unique assets which can be produced while maintaining the availability of more popular assets unlimited. Creators may also encode complex assets on-chain to ensure that they do not alter over time. This is incredibly fascinating in the case of art, which is highly dependent on the provable scarcity of an original object.

Programmability

Of course, NFTs are entirely programmable, much like conventional virtual properties. CryptoKitties built a breeding mechanism right into the contract that reflects the virtual cats. Many modern NFTs have more advanced technologies, such as forging, crafting, redeeming, random creation, and so on. The design world is brimming with possibilities.

Standards for Non-Fungible Tokens

Non-fungible tokens are practical because of their standards. They provide creators with the assurance that products will behave in a particular manner and detail how to communicate with the products' core functionality.

ERC721

What is ERC-721?

The ERC-721 provides a standard for NFT, which means that this form of Token is unique and may have a higher value than another Token from the same Smart Contract, for example, due to its age, rarity, or even its visual. Hold on, visual? Yeah, indeed! Since all NFTs have a uint256 variable named tokenId, the pair contract address, uint256 tokenId, should be generally unique for every ERC-721 Contract. A dApp may have a "converter" that takes the tokenId as input and returns an image of something interesting, such as zombies, guns, abilities, or awesome kitties!

The ERC-721 (Ethereum Request for Comments 721) is a Non-Fungible Token Standard that incorporates an API for tokens inside Smart Contracts, as introduced by William Entriken, Dieter Shirley, Jacob Evans, and Nastassia Sachs in January 2018. It involves features such as moving tokens between one account to another, obtaining an account's current token balance, obtaining the holder of a given token, and obtaining the total supply of a token presence on the network. It does have some other features, such as approving the transfer of a certain amount of token from one account to a third-party account.

ERC721 was the pioneering standard for describing non-fungible virtual products, and CryptoKitties created it. Since ERC721 is an inheritable Solidity smart contract standard, creators can quickly build new ERC721-compliant contracts by simply extracting them from the OpenZeppelin library. ERC721 is basically very easy: it maps unique identifiers (which each involves a specific product) to addresses representing the identifier's holder. The transferFrom approach in ERC721 also offers a permission way to transfer these properties.

When you reflect on it, these two methods are all that's needed to describe an NFT: a way to determine who holds what and a manner to pass items around. There are a few other features in the standard (many of which are crucial for NFT markets). However, the core of ERC721 is rather simple.

ERC1155

The Enjin team pioneered ERC1155, which introduces the concept of semi-fungibility to the world of NFTs. IDs in ERC1155 reflect asset groups rather than single properties. For instance, an ID could denote "swords," and a wallet may contain 1,000 swords. The balance of method, in this situation, would return the number of swords possessed by a wallet, and a user could pass on any number of swords by calling transferFrom with the "sword" ID.

One benefit of this approach is efficiency: with ERC721, if a holder wanted to transfer 1,000 swords, they'd have to change the smart contract's status (by calling the transferFrom strategy) for 1,000 different tokens. The creator just needs to call transferFrom with a quantity of 1,000 and conduct a single transfer process with ERC1155. Of course, improved productivity comes at the cost of knowledge loss: we can no longer track the past of a single sword.

Also, since ERC1155 is a superset of ERC721 features, an ERC721 product may be created with ERC1155 (you'd just need a different ID and quantity 1 for every product). Because of these benefits, the ERC1155 standard has progressively seen increased adoption. OpenSea recently created a Github platform to help people get started with the ERC1155 standard.

Composables

Composables, led by the ERC-998 standard, provides a framework for non-fungible and fungible properties owned by NFTs. While there have only been a few composable NFTs launched, we believe there are a lot of exciting applications for them! A cryptokitty might have a scratching post and a feeding bowl, with the latter containing fungible "chow" tokens. If I sell the cryptokitty, I also sell all of the cryptokitty's possessions.

Non-Ethereum Standards

Though Ethereum is presently the center of attention, many other NFT standards are gaining traction on other chains. Beginning with EOS, DGoods, which was created by the Mythical Games team, aims to provide a feature-rich cross-chain standard. The Cosmos project is already working on an NFT component that will be included in the Cosmos SDK.

Non-Fungible Token Metadata

On any marketplace, the owner of the method helps you to find out who owns an NFT. Take for instance, the owner of CryptoKitty #1500718 at the time of writing is a user with the address 0x6452 by querying ownerOf(1500718) on the CryptoKitties smart contract. But how do OpenSea and CryptoKitties, for example, determine the appearance of CryptoKitty #1500718? What regarding its name and distinguishing characteristics?

This is where metadata enters the picture. For a given token ID, metadata offers specific information. The name of the cat, an image of the cat, a summary, and further additional characteristics (called "cattributes" in the context of CryptoKitties) make up the metadata. The date of the event and the type of ticket, as well as a name and summary, may be included in the metadata for an event ticket.

Therefore, the concern is how and where to preserve this data so that NFT-related applications can obtain it.

On-chain vs. Off-chain

The first decision creators to make is whether to reflect metadata on-chain or off-chain. Do you include the metadata in the smart contract that represents the tokens, or do you keep it separate?

On-chain Metadata

The advantages of storing metadata on-chain are that 1) it is permanently associated with the token, lasting beyond the lifespan of any specific application, and 2) it can be modified according to on-chain logic. If products are meant to have long-term value beyond their original development, point #1 is critical. A piece of virtual artwork, for instance, is supposed to last through the years, irrespective of whether the initial website that was used to produce the artwork is still operational. As a consequence, its metadata must survive the token identifier's lifespan.

On-chain logic will also need to communicate with metadata. For instance, in the case of CryptoKitties, a CryptoKitty's "generation" determines how easily it can reproduce, and breeding takes place entirely on the blockchain (higher generation cats reproduce more slowly). As a result, the smart contract's logic must be able to read metadata from its internal state.

Off-chain Metadata

Despite these advantages, many projects store their metadata off-chain owing to the Ethereum blockchain's existing storage constraints. As a result, the ERC721 specification provides a tokenURI method that creators can use to tell applications where to look for metadata for a specific asset.

The tokenURI process returns a public URL. This, in effect, produces a JSON dictionary of data. For applications like OpenSea to recognize this metadata, it must adhere to the official ERC721 metadata standard. We like creators to construct rich metadata that can be shown inside the marketplace, with added extensions to the ERC721 metadata specification that enable them to include attributes, animations, and background colors.

Centralized Servers

The most straightforward approach to store metadata is on a centralized server or in a cloud storage service like AWS. Of course, there are drawbacks: 1) The metadata may be changed at any time by the creator; 2) If the project is taken offline, the metadata can be lost. To address problem 2, some providers are now caching metadata on their own servers to make sure that it can be delivered to users reliably even when the original hosting solution falls down.

IPFS

The InterPlanetary File System (IPFS) is being used by a growing number of developers, especially in the virtual art space, to store metadata off-chain. IPFS is a peer-to-peer file storage framework that distributes content through several devices, allowing it to be reproduced in multiple locations. This means that A) the metadata is permanent because the file's hash represents explicitly it, and B) the data will survive over time as long as there are nodes ready to support it. Creators will now use services like Pinata to manage the framework for deploying and maintaining IPFS nodes, and the much-anticipated Filecoin network would (in theory) add a layer on top of IPFS to incentivize nodes to host data.

Chapter 12:
START YOUR NFTs BUSINESS

NFTs Ownership

NFTs are currently all the rage, but buyers and sellers should be mindful of the various regulatory mechanisms that could apply to these properties. While this isn't an NFT, you wouldn't be surprised if it had been.

- **NFTs and Intellectual Property Law**

NFTs are now commonplace. But how do they fit into the laws and regulations that already exist? Why it matters?

NFTs are gaining traction, although it's uncertain how they'll fit into the legal and regulatory structures that regulate the financial, technology, and cryptocurrency sectors. Since NFTs are not the same as initial coin offerings (ICOs), they cannot be regarded as a security. Although laws are governing NFT operations' conduct, it is critical to ensure that customers are mindful of their actions.

- **Breaking it down**

NFTs are the type of digital collectibles. They can represent objects (such as tweets, real estate, and other tangible assets), or they can be things themselves like art (as discussed in previous chapters). Their value proposition is that they are virtually identical, live on a blockchain (such as Ethereum), and while anyone can duplicate and import video clips or image files, an NFT has a history that has solely one owner. To be clear, the image file stored in an NFT could still be downloaded. If you sell a tweet, it will stay available to everyone on Twitter. In that sense, you're buying a virtually validated note rather than the tweet itself. They're close to autographed football cards. You can print as many cards as you wish. However, if the player only signs one, it will most probably be the most valuable card. An autographed Tom Brady card, for instance, recently sold for $1.32 million.

According to Carlton Fields ' Andrew Hinkes, we might just be scratching the surface of what NFTs can do. An NFT, at the most basic level, can recognize a specific financial property that can result in new efficiencies in current transactions. One example is land ownership: at the moment, people rely on land registries held by third parties, such as a government department, to show that they own a plot of land. An NFT, according to Hinkes, could be used to identify the property, allowing a person to prove ownership with a cryptographically protected and signed digital token.

Fabrica's Daniel Rollingher, a real estate attorney, pointed out that real estate NFTs may require consumers to borrow from lenders, requiring NFT issuers to adhere to consumer protection and disclosure regulations.

Holder Protection

One of the problems with NFTs, according to Donna Redel, a panel member of the New York Angels and an associate professor at Fordham Law, is that several customers may have no idea what they're purchasing. Besides that, NFTs pose additional concerns about who is conducting know-your-customer/anti-money laundering practices, which is really documenting the selling of an NFT, and the rights buyers have.

"I'm not sure the artists understand their rights and responsibilities, both under the contract and in the wider, more legal world," she said. "I expect to see more stuff like [NBA] Top Shot, which is a walled garden." According to Andrew Jacobson of Seward and Kissel, NFTs have become especially popular with a younger, less educated audience.

- **Law**

NFTs, according to Jacobson, could run afoul of nation's sanctions law, which prohibits residents and people from doing business with individuals or entities from sanctioned countries. However, there could be an exemption for information and information content, allowing citizens to interact with artwork from sanctioned countries. What if you had an NFT that emerged in Iran, North Korea, or another sanctioned country... how would you handle it from a sanctions standpoint?

There's also a possibility that malicious actors will see NFTs as a way to raise or launder money, he said, citing the Marine Chain ICO as an instance of how a sanctioned organization has tried to secure funding in the past through cryptocurrencies. I believe platforms that offer, process, or create NFTs should take that into account. Platforms must also be careful not to be confused by money transfer companies.

Since Financial rules regulate items that substitute for value, you might argue that an NFT is a valuable substitute. Financial regulations don't care about the asset; they think about people and conduct.

- **Intellectual Property and Copyright**

The question is if buyers' expectations of what they purchased match the legal truth. Sellers, especially established companies that are jumping on the bandwagon face the same problem. Sellers must also ensure that the NFT they sell contains the exact material they wish to sell; unlike most virtual files, an NFT cannot be easily edited after being registered on a blockchain.

You can't undo anything; there's no turning back." You can issue a second token, but the original NFT will remain in circulation, so you must understand and be aware of any possible risks. There are also concerns about how NFTs could interact with current copyright legislation. "There's no one who's serious about NFTs who actually humors the notion that what you're selling is the copyright or the master suggesting that the artists maintain the copyright while selling some kind of licensed material to buyers.

Although musicians and artists who mint NFTs of their own work are likely to be aware of their rights, anyone can mint NFTs of works they did not make. I'm curious whether the new NFT platforms on the market have policies and procedures in place to handle that possibility. What if anyone on OpenSea minted a bunch of Mickey Mouse-related NFTs, and then Walt Disney lawyers contacted the platform?

- **Counterfeiting**

Many NFTs represent real-world objects, which increases the risk of the connection between the real-world object and the NFT that means it is broken. The real thing that might arise is that you sell something on a platform and claim that it's an NFT that resides on a blockchain, which is false. Many users will have no idea of verifying whether that is real or false as they aren't smart enough to check. "The products could either not be an NFT at all, just a cool-looking picture, or an NFT that is linked to a different blockchain.

- ## Securities and Taxation Rules

NFTs could run afoul of securities laws, but this appears to be less realistic than most of the other regulatory regimes in which they deal. An individual who purchases an NFT with the assumption that it will increase in value will sue the creator of the NFT actually decreases in value. I believe it is similar in that there is a lot of public demand, but traditional securities, sanctions, and commodity legislation would have to be readjusted.

Buyers of NFTs may often have to contend with various tax laws in different jurisdictions. When NFTs are linked to art, the buyer typically has to deal with this problem. Who is in charge of collecting sales tax? Somebody has to pay sales tax when you purchase $4.6 million worth of art, and it's the buyer's responsibility.

Chapter 13:
USING THE MARKETPLACE

Rarible NFT Marketplace

Crypto art's rise was one of the most intriguing developments of 2020, and it shows no signs of slowing down as we head into 2021. NFT art marketplaces like Rarible have exploded on Ethereum, thanks in part to the massive amount of value created by the DeFi dapp operation. In light of this, it's maybe appropriate that Rarible established its reputation by using a key DeFi technique. Anyone who sells or buys art on Rarible receives a portion of the 75,000 RARI tokens issued weekly to promote action. Definitely, this is simply another type of asset or yield farming, which began with the introduction of Compound's COMP token in June.

The great news is that it has prompted more individuals to use Rarible and begin collecting crypto art, leading to Rarible becoming a regular fixture in DappRadar's top three platform dapp rankings.

- **Minting NFTs**

People like Rarible because it enables everyone to create an NFT artwork for a small fee. Although some sites, such as SuperRare and Makers Place, curate their artists, anyone can build an NFT on Rarible. This opened the way for emerging talent and aspiring artists, though it also opened the ay for fraudsters. To tackle the possibility of dealing with a fake project, Rarible has developed a verification system.

How to Make Your Own Nft On Rarible

- Link your wallet to Rarible.com (i.e., Metamask)
- At the top of the page, select the blue CREATE option.
- Choose whether you like to create a single NFT or several editions of an NFT.
- Upload a picture, a video, or a piece of music.
- Include a price, a name, a description, royalties, and any other relevant information.
- Build a new item by clicking the button.

You'll be asked to sign and pay for gas in your pocket. Gas prices can be expensive, so it's worth it to time your NFT minting.

SuperRare Marketplace

- **Meaning of SuperRare Marketplace**

SuperRare is a website whereby artists produce artwork that is combined with a token that is as exclusive as the artwork itself. SuperRare is a blockchain-based social network for art creators and owners. On the Ethereum blockchain, artists can mint digital artworks and tokenize them. Smart contracts allow collectors to buy and sell artworks while royalties are returned to the artist. There's more to crypto-collectibles than cartoon kittens. SuperRare makes digital art rare–provably rare–by harnessing the Ethereum blockchain's strength.

Individuals want the real deal when it comes to collectibles, and they are ready to spend a lot of money on it. And where there's big money, there's also theft, forgery, and other mischiefs. The whole history and source of a work of art can be traced using the Ethereum blockchain, a distributed ledger that no one owns and can access.

Artists develop a work of art and tokenize it on the SuperRare network, which means they connect the art to a token. The new digital art is inextricably linked to a Non-Fungible Token, and it's not just any token (NFT). This particular Ethereum token has the quality of being as one-of-a-kind as the artwork.

The NFT can be purchased, leased, or even held as a future investment once it is on SuperRare. Artists have the option of putting their work up for sale or selling it for a fixed price. The NFT can then be resold at any price on a number of NFT trading sites after it has been sold to a buyer.

- **What Makes It So Unique**

SuperRare is a website that connects digital art collectors and allows them to "social collect." SuperRare was founded on the premise that collecting is inherently social and that collectors and artists should easily engage through their common interests. Users will see who the top collectors and trending artists are, as well as how many items they've purchased or made and how much ETH they've invested or accumulated on the site. You can also see the artwork itself, as well as a summary and a biography of its previous owners.

How to Create SuperRare Tokens

While everyone may buy and keep Ethereum tokens like the NFTs SuperRare, only invited artists may mint artwork on the marketplace. To become a member of the network as an artist, you will complete an application that specifies that specific artwork created for SuperRare would have to be original, produced by you, digital, and not tokenized anywhere else on the web.

How to Buy SuperRare Artwork

All SuperRare transactions must be performed in Ethereum that can be bought on any cryptocurrency platform. Users will have to bind to the SuperRare network using MetaMask in order to communicate.

For the ethereum - based blockchain technology, AtomicAssets is a new Non-Fungible Token (NFT) platform. It addresses existing standards' usability problems by demanding no RAM from the user while also providing unique tools such as native two-sided exchange offers and token-backed NFTs. It is also very RAM effective.

AtomicAsset Marketplace

AtomicAssets is exciting for someone who isn't a nerd in the digital world. The majority of AtomicAssets' features explicitly contribute to a better service for users, even if they aren't conscious of it.

Users do not have to pay for RAM. And, when you think about it, this shouldn't come as a surprise. The notion of requiring blockchain services to communicate with a webpage is something that most people are unfamiliar with. You don't have to pay for each transfer you attempt on Steam or each WhatsApp text you send. It's why, with AtomicAssets, the NFT creator just has to pay for RAM once, whenever minting the product, and then you don't have to worry about it anymore.

How to Mint On Atomic Asset

Anyone can make their own collections and mint their own NFTs using the NFT Creator, requiring no programming experience.

- Creating a Collection is the first step. Collections serve as a container for NFTs with similar themes, such as those belonging to the same Dapp.

- The development of a Schema is the next step. Schemas are associated with a set, and a collection may contain several schemas. They decide which characteristics the assets would have (in tech terms: the data structure). Series 1 could be a schema in the GPK example, and the attributes could be Name, Image, ID, Variant, Rarity, and Mint Number.

- The third step is not necessary, but it can be beneficial. It's the process of constructing a Template that belongs to a specific schema. A schema may have several templates once again. Consider a prototype to be a set of predefined features. Products will later refer to a template and have the template's feature values applied to them automatically. Templates may also have a limited supply, giving NFTs a measurable scarcity. In the case of GPK, you might make one design for each card variation. For example, a template may describe the following values:

- "Fryin' Brian" is the name of the character.

- Illustration: An IPFS Hash

- 4 ID

- "A" variant

- "Golden" rarity

Set a cap of 25 for the supply.

- The asset is created in the final phase (NFT). Assets are often part of a collection. You set the values of the features that were initially specified in the schema when constructing the product.

As previously discussed, assets may also reference a template, wherein the template's values are added to the product automatically. You might, for example, build 25 assets in GPK that all reference the "Fryin' Brian" template. Since all of the other features have already been set in the template, you'd just have to change the value of the Mint Number feature.

Walking through those procedures for the first time is definitely not very user-friendly. Nevertheless, we agree that the advantages of this more streamlined structure exceed the extra 5 minutes or so required to produce your first NFT. Bear in mind that collections and schemas only need to be generated once, and they can then be reused in the future.

Decentraland Marketplace

What You Can Do with The Marketplace

The following features are available on the Marketplace:

- Define your own price in MANA and a deadline for the bid when you publish a piece of LAND for sale.
- Purchase a for-sale parcel.
- Offer your package a name and a description.

- Move your LAND to a separate user.
- You can keep track of the parcels you own and see how much you've contributed to districts.
- See who controls everything by looking at a map of the planet.

How to Secure Your Assets

The Marketplace platform is supported by a smart contract that allows users to buy and sell LAND in a secure and reliable manner. The Marketplace is fully open source, and the contract code is available on GitHub.

We've equally made the Marketplace easy to use for atomic swaps. An atomic swap is a deal in cryptocurrency trading that needs each entity to meet their obligation (either providing MANA or a LAND token) within a certain period. The transaction is considered complete if and only if each entity fulfills its responsibilities before the time limit expires. All of this is done by an Ethereum smart contract. These atomic swaps eliminate all counterparty risks.

How to Use Decentraland

Visit market.decentraland.org to get acquainted with the Marketplace, reading over our Terms & Conditions, and begin browsing LAND in the Atlas!

You'll need to log in and activate your wallet when you're ready to start trading or viewing your LAND holdings. The Marketplace accepts hardware wallets from MetaMask, Mist, and Ledger. If you've previously bought LAND, ensure you're using the same wallet address you used during the LAND sale, or the lands won't appear in your wallet.

Management of Your Land

This section was created to help you handle all of your Landed properties. Click My Land to see this entry. You'll find a list of all of your plots here, including those you've donated to public districts and those you've marked for sale.

You may modify the name, description, put it up for sale, or move it straight to another account address by clicking on one of the parcels described under My Land.

Dealing with Purchase

You must first allow the Marketplace to conduct safe trades for your wallet from the settings page before you can trade LAND. You're ready to trade once you've given the Marketplace permission to run MANA and LAND on your behalf. Decentraland doesn't really receive any surplus trading costs, apart from the small gas fee charged by miners for each transaction on the Ethereum platform.

If you have another wallet to which you like to pass your LAND, or if you wish to give LAND to a friend without costing them MANA, you can do so by clicking Transfer on the parcel's tab.

KnownOrigin Marketplace

How It Works

It offers artists a safe forum to display and sell their work and backed by a public blockchain solution.

Applying to Be an Artist

To join KnownOrigin as an artist or author, you must first create a profile page. This normally consists of a profile image, bio, and social media accounts such as Twitter and Instagram to develop a strong following, and it is achieved through the Sign-in tab. Before doing so, artists would need to download a digital wallet such as MetaMask.io or TrustWallet. After you've built a profile, you can apply using the Artist application form. KnownOrigin spends time going through the applications and confirming the artists' identities through direct contact on Instagram, Twitter, and email. They aim to maintain a high degree of due diligence, affecting the time it takes to introduce new artists to the website.

Creating Digital Artwork

Artists create digital artwork that KnownOrigin can tokenize. All artwork files are stored on IPFS (a distributed storage system), and each product is assigned a unique identifier that can be monitored for chain-of-custody and authenticity purposes.

Upload Art to Gallery

The artist retains full control over the number of copies available, resulting in scarcity. There will be no more products generated until all of the products have been sold. Using blockchain technology, all-digital artwork can be tracked in real-time, and anybody can see the transaction history.

Selling Rare Digital Artwork

NFTs (non-fungible tokens) minted by the KnownOrigin smart contract is available for purchase by owners. They are a commission-based network, and this is built into the smart contract, so there are no intermediaries to deal with, and artists will be paid directly for their hard work and talent.

Chapter 14:
HOW TO BE AN NFT ARTIST

Music

Building an Online Following

I t's critical to think about what you'll need to bring up and where it will all live online when you begin to prepare and plan to start your digital business. Will a record label or a concert promoter be able to find out what they need to learn about you without much effort? Or would they have to sift through a jumble of loose ends, random profiles, and probably broken ties to hear your music and get a sense of what you're up to?

- **Electronic Press Kit(EPK)**

EPK, short for the electronic press kit. EPK refers to a pre-packaged collection of advertising materials sent to a fanbase for promotional purposes. They are often circulated to publicize a new release. EPKs produce and distribute electronic press kits to media platforms, assisting large and small businesses and individuals in getting heard. Media people (editors, writers, radio show managers, venue talent buyers, and so on) can quickly locate all of your products, such as image and music files, bios, and so on, via your electronic press kit. The following elements should be included:

- **Bio**

While no one requires a book, a successful bio must contain certain elements. Although I can't tell you how to write the best artist bio for your profile, I can provide you primary elements and not include them in your bio.

The following are essential components to include:

Professional experience

Exhibition highlights

Highlights of the Award

Highlights of professional life

Your work's elevator pitch

Describe your journey to becoming a professional artist in a few words.

Two or three pictures of you working in your studio

What not to avoid:

Bloviating

Technical artspeak

Highlighting every single exhibition and award you've got.

Being to salesy

- **Your Image**

Get Professional photos taken. Now Photography doesn't have to be expensive, and yet it can make a big difference. Provide writers and editors with a link to high-resolution images, think Google Drive or Dropbox. If required, provide photo credit details.

- **Quotes from the Public**

Add some positive quotes if you've been published on the net or in print. If not, don't worry; after all, that is the reason you're pitching!

- **Your Art/Music Links**

Please take into account that everyone has their own favorite outlets, including major streaming services such as Itunes, as well as Netlabel and/or Soundcloud.

- **Social Media/Website Profiles**

You don't have to worry much about promotion since that is what social media marketing for artists entails. Is there a new song? Is there a new album on the way? Let your fanbase know! Putting together frequent fliers and announcements, which are ideal for pinned tweets or messages, is a good move. Anyone who visits your profile will be able to see just what you're up to.

Also, keep in mind that social selling is entirely legal for artists. You can sell your merch on social media with no embarrassment if you use imaginative ads and sales. Also, bear in mind that your fans can be a great source of content. Enabling user-generated content in the form of tagged fan images is a fantastic way to engage with fans while also showing them some love. Reposting these images is a subtle but effective way to strengthen your relationship with your audience and show them you care.

If you're constantly touring or playing shows and aren't sure how to effectively promote your music on Twitter, start by thanking your fans and sharing images from your shows. On a similar note, credibility is an essential element of social media marketing for artists.

It's also beneficial to engage with your followers personally instead of only posting promo after promo. Posting content that takes your fans behind the scenes is an added plus. Tagging is a well-known way to quickly improve your posts' popularity on Facebook, Twitter, and Instagram. As a result, tagging others in your posts when needed is always a good idea.

Announcing a location where you'll be performing, highlighting other artists you're on tour with, or an album you're covering may appear counterintuitive but don't underestimate the value of communicating with fans. Perhaps they enjoy your new album. Maybe they have a question about your most recent release. Responding and retweeting demonstrates that you're paying attention to what they're saying. Although it might not seem important to you, shout-outs will make fans feel like celebrities and inspire them to become even more devoted fans in the long run.

Your Website

With social networking sites providing many ways to interact with our favorite artists, making a website can seem outdated for many people. Nevertheless, by developing an artist website, you're establishing a central location where all of the knowledge shared through these social networks can be found. While an EPK can be found on an artist's website, the two are not inherently synonymous. Consider a website as being more fan-focused, whereas an EPK is more business-focused. Individuals that want to cover your music and individuals that want to connect as fans, accept it or not, will find sites very useful.

However, an artist's website could be more than simply a repository for links and photographs. Creating a website is just the beginning; what you wish to do with your website is entirely up to you. Perhaps it's to advertise concert dates, or maybe it's to collect more contact details from fans. Whatever your goal is, you should make it the focal point of your website. Fortunately, there is a multitude of tools available to make designing and managing a website simple. WordPress is a straightforward one to manage.

How to Create a WordPress Artist Website

Deciding on a theme for your website is a vital part of getting started. Since the theme determines your website's design, it's critical to choose one with an appealing design that complements your band's style. There are a few more steps to take after you've chosen the desired theme before we start building your website. You'll have to purchase a domain name as well as a hosting plan on which to install WordPress and your chosen theme.

1. Choose a domain name

Your domain is the address where your fans can find your website on the internet. If possible, purchase a domain with exact spelling as your band's name and a.COM extension. If your desired name is already taken, you can add a word like "gang" or "live."

2. Choose a Hosting Plan

The next move is to choose a web hosting provider. There is a slew of hosting providers that sell low-cost monthly plans. Try Envato Hosted if you're not sure where to begin. Premium controlled WordPress hosting is available from Envato Hosted for USD 19 per month (+ relevant taxes).

3. Plan the content for your website

It's a great idea to compile and plan all of the album tracks, cover art, band member bios, and everything else you like to add on your website when it comes to content. In the nearest future, this would save you time since many themes have sample content that you can adopt to easily set up your website before replacing it with your own.

How to Build Your Artist Website

It's time to get started on your website now that you've done the steps above. The first move is to download and install WordPress. After that, you can install your theme and any necessary plugins and proceed with theme setup and customization.

Install WordPress

Firstly, begin by installing WordPress. You will receive a welcome email from your hosting with information about your purchased plan, as well as your username, password, and connection to your account's control panel. To log in, click the link in the email and enter the login information given.

Check for the WordPress icon in the Website or Scripts section after signing in. Follow the onscreen directions after pressing the button. Fill in your website title, description, username, password, and email address as directed by the prompts. Then, press the Install button. To access your website, simply go to www.yoursitename.com/wp-admin and enter the username and password you set up during the installation.

Create a WordPress Music Theme

Go to Appearance > Themes > Add new to install the theme you purchased. Then choose Upload Theme from the drop-down menu. After that, locate and upload the zipped folder containing the theme's files; after you've completed the installation, press Activate.

Install the WordPress Plugins required

After you activate the theme, you'll see a message in your dashboard stating that some plugins are needed for the theme to run properly. A connection will be provided that will take you straight to the installation screen. Click Install after choosing all of the plugins. After that, the plugins will begin installing, and your website will become active right away.

- **Profiles on Social Media**

Many music lovers are now on online media sites such as Facebook, Twitter, YouTube, Instagram, and Snapchat in some capacity. When your music career progresses, you'll discover that social networking is an excellent way to communicate (and stay connected) with your fans.

To learn more above social media following, go to the TuneCore Social Media Beginner's Guide for a step-by-step guide to acquiring, developing, and engaging with followers that will teach you everything you need to know about:

Creating Your Personal Brand

- Interacting with fans, venues, and other brands, among other things
- Differentiation of channels
- Analyses of social media
- Posts that have been boosted and advertisements

You'll start to learn the type of content sharing that fits for you after you've established your social media following (which might involve choosing which sites to avoid based on the type of audiences you're planning to reach). It has a lot to do with discovering your "social voice" and intonation, though it equally has a lot to do with simple experimentation, so have fun with it!

Email List

In a fast-changing world, email was one of the first significant developments connected with the digital age, and as a result, it could be considered "old school." Irrespective, email lists may have a significant influence on musicians. Yes, posting or writing a direct message to audiences may appear to be the most straightforward way to connect with them. However, music fans, like anyone else, monitor their email inboxes as well. Furthermore, email has the most robust user engagement per message. Fans are more inclined to go over an email than a Social media post, which is digital overload of content.

First and foremost, figure out how to expand your email list. Two of the best approaches here are providing bonuses in return for your supporters' email addresses and setting up a sign-up page at your promotional table. In return for a supporter's email address, you can provide free downloads or access to exclusive content. A realistic solution is to offer new fans with tiny, free pieces of products at your table after a show in return for their email addresses being added to your mailing list.

Once you've started building your email list, and don't stress if it's tiny at first; Rome wasn't built in a day, after all. It's time to decide what type of content you'd like to share. Whenever it comes to sharing great information about a new album, a concert, a music video, or a radio/TV show, email lists offer a simple, broad-reaching contact option. Still, they can equally be used to simply check-in and say hi to your followers, making them aware you're always thinking about them. As with anything else, it's vital not to misuse such lists or render the emails you send too repetitive. Music fans, like you, won't like to be spammed.

Consider it from the perspective of what you'd share on social media. Individuals that open your mails are a few of your most devoted followers, so send them something that will entice them to read your subsequent one. Here are a few suggestions:

- Singles or early entry to events
- Views from behind the scenes
- Announcements of concert dates and shows
- Fresh merchandise is available for purchase.
- This one may be able to give you a special discount!

Put in some effort into the quality of your newsletters, and build and develop a 'tone' that your supporters will relate to and appreciate, just as you do with your social media accounts. Creating and keeping to an email schedule will help you from going overboard or missing essential emails. Did we note that in terms of e-commerce, email is more efficient per supporter than social networks? When you're prepared, begin setting some sales targets to track your progress in this field. Remember to strike a balance and avoid coming across as pushy.

Pitching Your Music

Simply because you produced a fantastic single, EP, or album doesn't imply everybody will know about it. Sure, you've contacted your friends and relatives, shared on social media, made the products available on your website, and shared links to digital stores and streaming services. However, If you think the digital marketing activities are finished after that, think again.

If you wish to follow in the footsteps of your favorite artists and get your songs displayed on playlists, podcasts, and regional digital channels, you'll have to pitch it! While you will eventually want to hire a publicist for this type of job, don't be misled, you can simply pitch yourself.

Playlists

As streaming continues to attract an increasing number of listeners, channels such as Apple Music and Spotify have developed methods to provide these fans with curated playlists of music they might enjoy or, in most cases, may not even realize they want. That's why streaming has paved the way for new musical experimentation stages, and emerging artists aren't left out!

Some things can be done as a new digital artist, and try to get your songs included on any of these playlists. First and foremost, ensure you're approved on any sites where you can upload images and create profiles. Then, to remind folks where they can locate you and connect you to their individual playlists, you can promote your streaming network links on social media, your website, and in emails.

Pitching to lesser-known, unofficial playlists is a technique that certain musicians have ignored. For instance, while we're all familiar with Spotify's "Rap Caviar," there is a slew of "unofficial" Spotify curators who curate playlists with sizable (and committed) followings. Follow such people on social media and tell them what you like about their playlists and the reason your latest single will be a perfect addition. Try not to spam, to be courteous, and do not expect an answer all of the time.

Also, if you're using TuneCore to distribute your new music and give yourself at least three weeks' notice, you can use our Feature Release form, which is sent to editorial teams through digital stores.

Online Outlets and Websites

If you're a musician, it's possible that you're also a music lover with favorite online outlets for exploring new music. Music-related blogs and online magazines could be a perfect way to attract new people to like your music. As previously said, you could get underway on these initiatives without spending on a publicist early in your music career. It simply takes some effort.

To begin, carve out time for analysis, a lot of it. Look for blogs and other websites that want to display the type of music you create on the net (and ensure the websites are frequently updated, too). Although they might not make it simple, you ought to be able to find general contact details or, in some instances, clear "Submission Guidelines" on the web.

Create a strong media list, and where possible, check out different writers who tend to be lovers of your style (one tip is to search for writers who have covered artists with whom you'd equate your style, this will give you something to link to in the promotional email), It will make them learn more about you if you give them the EPK you learned about above.

When pitching to writers and websites, keep in mind that it's vital not to get frustrated or depressed. If you don't hear back after one try, respect the inboxes of the people you're pitching to, and don't take it to heart.

Digital Art

How to Become a Digital Artist

If you have the creative skill and cherish drawing and painting, this could be a very satisfying and low-stress way to supplement your income on a temporary basis. Furthermore, knowing how to make digital art is just one of the many relevant skills that can assist you with various other revenue streams and side hustles.

So, where do you begin with digital art? What equipment do you require? And how do you go about finding work? Let's take a look.

- What you need to get started with digital art is the right hardware

You'll require specific hardware and software to begin your digital art journey. Many digital artists prefer to use a graphics tablet from a company such as Wacom. This is a simple slate that plugs into a computer and comes with a stylus. According to the concept, you can now draw straight on the tablet and see your art appear on the monitor. This gives you far more control than you'd get with a mouse.

Surface Pro 6

A tablet, like an iPad Pro or a Surface Pro, is another alternative. This has a lot of benefits, including the ability to draw straight on your art and the capacity to move your creations. Because of their sensitivity and marginal lag, digital artists prefer iPads and Surface Pros, which are rapidly becoming the de-facto alternative. Which of these techniques you choose may be determined by the software you intend to use (more on that in a moment).

You may use a Samsung Galaxy Tab or Note, and though software support is restricted. And the latter is a bit of a squeeze on the screen. The form of art you like to make will determine which program is best for you. With a mouse and keyboard, you can use various gadgets, and certain applications would be simpler to use this way, so you should also invest in a decent PC.

Vector art vs. Raster

After you've sorted out the hardware, it's time to move on to the software. The form of art you like to make will determine which program is best for you. This necessitates an understanding of the differences between raster and vector files.

A raster file is a bitmap image in which the pixels are plotted on a map. Most of the file formats you're likely acquainted with are included, such as JPG, GIF, and PNG. Because every pixel is a grid point, it's effortless to draw directly onto the image. Nevertheless, it equally means that editing the image without erasing entire sections is hard. Similarly, when you zoom in on an image, those points grow larger, resulting in pixilation. Because many search engines and operating systems promote raster images, they are widely used on the internet. They are, nevertheless, not particularly adaptable.

In contrast, a vector file functions more like a set of guidelines. Vector art is made up of many lines and curves, and the image saves information about all of these guidelines (move 30% across the image at an angle of 20 degrees, then curve at an angle) so that the image can be reproduced as needed.

This implies that you really can zoom in on the image while maintaining its quality. The guidelines have simply been scaled up to fit the larger canvas. You can also erase individual strokes or change angles without affecting the rest of the picture at any time. Designers who create logos will be required to provide vector files in addition to their completed raster images. A company's logo must be able to be reproduced at any size and edited while maintaining the exact roughly equivalent dimensions. Numerous digital artist jobs are similar, whether you're designing a print for a clothing piece or an icon for a user interface. Keep in mind that vector software is often less user-friendly and flexible. This implies that you may zoom in on the picture while maintaining its quality.

You may also come across other files that you need to deal with. Learning to build 3D models, for instance, will offer you an advantage. This will enable you to add a 3D component to your images, produce various types of art, and even generate reference images. Learning 3D isn't necessary anymore for many kinds of jobs, but it can help you stand out from the crowd, so it's strongly recommended.

The Best Digital Artist Software

With that in mind, here are a few apps that digital artists can use to get started:

Procreate

Install Procreate if you have an iPad Pro and need a tool that can enable you to get started with digital art rapidly and effortlessly. It's not cheap (around $15), though it's one of the most user-friendly and strong tools for creating incredible digital art.

Optimus Prime Drawing

Procreate is a raster image editor. It comes with a large variety of excellent brushes, numerous customization features, and the ability to work with large canvases and layers. This last point is particularly significant because it indicates you can explore without jeopardizing your previous work. You can equally trace over work you've produced on paper with a pen and then scanned in. The piece is made even faster by handy shortcuts (like double-finger tap to undo), and the software saves every single move, enabling you to download a video of your artwork at the end. It's a fantastic tool

Adobe Photoshop

For many digital artists, Photoshop is the only alternative. Not only does it come with a large number of brushes, strong layer management, and support for several devices and tablets, but also, it has all of the filters, actions, as well as other functions you'd expect from a photo retouching program. Those with the talent can develop some pretty stunning art from start to end in Photoshop. Gimp is a decent free option if you're considering a free option, but it lacks a lot of digital artist-centric functionality.

ArtRage

ArtRage is a bitmap graphics editor that functions similarly to Procreate. Unlike Procreate, however, this one is cross-platform, enabling Windows users to participate. It's compatible with both Android and the Samsung S Pen. It's a common choice for digital artists because of its versatility in supporting a variety of art genres, especially water-color drawings. For those just getting started, ArtRage Lite is a more affordable choice.

Krita

Another raster graphics editor with layers and brushes is Krita. It runs on Windows, Linux, and Mac OS X, but the fact that it is fully free software sets it apart.

Adobe Illustrator

If you're looking to create vector graphics, there's only one method that leaves a lasting impression: Adobe Illustrator. Illustrator is the de facto standard and has all of the functionality you'll require, so most tutorials will concentrate on it. However, other software, like Inkscape, can also be used to construct vector art.

Blender

Blender is one of the 3D modeling applications available for making 3D art. Blender is an excellent option because it is free software, and you can get it from Steam!

Design Doll

Design Doll is a simple software that allows you to produce digital art reference poses. It can also help you figure out uncomfortable viewpoints and angles. The free edition contains most features and allows you to export 3D models and flat PNG images. However, it is only available for Windows.

How to Improve Your Digital Art skills

I suggest getting an iPad and Procreate, or a Surface Pro and Krita/Art Rage to get started with digital art. After this, it's mostly a question of consistency and dedication: even if your creations aren't perfect at first, stick with it, and they'll improve! After you've mastered raster techniques, you should move on to vector art and 3D modeling.

You may speed up your learning by enrolling in a class or trying out any of SkillShare's free tutorials for unique software packages. You can as well find a lot of tutorials and "speed paintings" on YouTube that guide you through the whole act of making digital art (there are equally plenty of real-time clips). These are good for picking up hints and seeing how the pros work.

- **How Digital Artists Monetize**

But what if you can already draw and would like to learn how to work as a digital artist who is rewarded for their efforts? I was so taken with EH Macmillan's artwork that I paid for the permission to apply it in my designs! I was so taken with EH Macmillan's artwork that I contacted him and paid for the rights to use it in my designs! This is how digital art is done.

- **Magnitude of Earnings**

The latter question is challenging to answer since it is highly dependent on the nature of the art and the form of the client. According to Glassdoor, Digital Artists in the United Kingdom receive around £23,030 a year. That's about $31,760 in today's currency. This isn't much, but if you're a famous artist with a considerable following who can draw big clients and command a high rate, things can change quickly. These figures could be higher with the application of NFTs

Chapter 15:
NFTs APPLICATION

NFTs in Gaming Industry

This is where things start to get interesting. Consider our previous illustrations of individuals claiming ownership of original digital assets such as images, paintings, etc. What if players had the same degree of ownership over extremely rare or difficult-to-get in-game items? For this method to operate, players must have total control over their NFTs; otherwise, they are useless.

Players could buy NFTs to immortalize and celebrate their most impressive achievements and game pieces. Players will be able to hold and own one-of-a-kind or highly restricted stamped pieces. Consider something incredibly restricted that is tied to in-game challenges and events. Here are a few fantastic concepts that could be built together in the games:

- The group that is the first to clear the new raid is rewarded with an object.
- A special incentive is given to the first 1,000 players who engage in an event; no further variants of the incentive will ever be added to the game.

- Masterwork/curated objects from incredibly rare world drops, also known as "title cards."
- Weapons, items, or character skins with increased scarcity, cost, or value.
- NFTs are linked to long-running live-service games that prolong or improve both publishers' and players' lifespan and value.
- Players could bid on the game's commemorative play highlight reels from eSports teams to own a franchise history piece.
- Players and fans will receive a one-of-a-kind, authenticated eSports in-game pieces.
- Subscription tokens that are digitized and have a lasting value.
- Convert a significant amount of in-game money to an exchangeable NFT that can be used in real life.
- Make a digital token out of a large number of in-game product pieces.

Giving NFT owners as much control as possible and the opportunity to sell and realize a real-world profit from their assets is vital to this scheme's success.

NFTs and In-Game Economies

To design and create their NFT systems, a developer might wish to employ a well-known economist who knows digital scarcity.

With cryptocurrency technology, precisely NFTs, whole player-driven economies could be generated and promoted. While developers and publishers would need to be mindful of the legal and technical criteria for integrating NFTs into their games, the possibilities are vast.

NFTs in Gaming History

The real-money auction house that came bundled with Diablo 3 was widely regarded as a complete disappointment. However, it is one of the first real-world examples of a player-driven economy with real-world financial consequences. Diablo 3 was the first video game I ever enjoyed that had an economic impact on my bottom line, which was awesome.

When Diablo 3 was out, I was almost done with high school, and I earned over $200 selling things in Blizzard's real-money auction house. I also built a devoted character who uses magic-find to improve my chances of finding valuable things to sell.

NFTs Prospect in Gaming

So, how do we proceed from here? Who knows what will happen. Nevertheless, history has proven that even the gaming industry's titans aren't scared to take risks and bend the rules of how things are done. NFTs may be the next big thing in the gaming industry.

It'll be fascinating to see how NFTs break into gaming and eSports. However, if the latest global trend is any indicator, it'll happen sooner rather than later.

NFTs and The Music Industry

Non-Fungible-Tokens (NFTs) have had the music world quiet. Well, let's just say "excited" in recent days. The numbers were staggering, and the headlines were breathless. In only 20 minutes, Grimes was able to sell $5.8 million in NFTs. For $11.6 million, 3lau sold 33 NFTs! T-former Mobile's CEO paid Steve Aoki $888,888.88 for an NFT titled "Hairy"! PERFECT! The rumor mill is accurate. Clubhouse is home to many NFT and crypto-art clubs, with several Twitter threads of people shouting at each other about the true existence of NFTs.

Experienced thought-leaders in the music industry believe NFTs are crucial. Speaking at the NY:LON Connect conference in January, Shara Senderoff, president of music/tech investment firm Raised In Space, accurately guessed that NFTS would "explode" owing to the "willingness for a fan to buy a product that is scarce, limited, and has prospective offerings attached to it that make them as a loyal fan feel special and compensated."

On the Pro-NFT side presently, there are a considerable buzz, cash, and opinions to be heard, and we're covering those perspectives. What, on the other hand, is the alternative viewpoint? Is there a possibility that this will become another ICO (initial coin offering) bubble like the one that occurred in 2017? What if people are dipping their toes into a technology they are unfamiliar with? WTF NFTs?

We asked two people who work closely with entertainment and blockchain technology a fundamental question: what's the other end of all this buzz?

Their responses weren't entirely critical, but they provided an alternate, stunning viewpoint on the ongoing frenzy of exaggerations and multimillion-dollar figures. When blockchain technology is hyped up like this, their general message is to be cautious.

NFTs to Music Industry

Simply put, you can release your music as an NFT in addition to existing platforms such as Spotify, Bandcamp, and anywhere else. Another advantage of NFTs is that they can take multiple forms and do not have to be entirely owned by a single person.

Let's pretend you're a rising star who's about to release your first album. You may make a one-of-a-kind NFT that reflects the entire album and thus becomes a collectible object. Now, the album will have unique content that is only available to one valid owner. For instance, they might receive a percentage of all album sales in perpetuity, a hidden single, or exclusive backstage access to your shows. You get to choose which features to include, and it's simple to set up.

Benefits to the Artist

You start by hosting an album sale on sites like Foundation or OpenSea or whichever marketplace you so desire, where your fans can bid on your collectible. Suppose the song becomes a smash, and one lucky fan that purchased the collectible and backed you gets to share in your success and all the rewards that follow.

You may also profit from reselling by including a percentage in the contract for any reselling of your collectible. So, if your NFT, which reflects your album, becomes a major success and is sold for huge amounts of money, later on, the artist will continue to be rewarded every time these transactions occur.

Advantages to the Collector

By taking out the middleman, they can help their favorite artists in a more significant, more intimate, and powerful way than they do through other services like Patreon. They will also be able to invest in the artwork. As a result, if the artist's career takes off, so does their collection. It turns into both a fascinating investment option and a show of support.

How to Get Started

It's now relatively simple to have your music minted and stored on the blockchain. In reality, when you have enough ether, you can tokenize and transform your music into a collectible NFT in a matter of a few minutes.

Setting Up Your NFTs Album, Ep, Or Track

- The first step is to obtain a free and stable cryptocurrency wallet. As previously described in the past chapter, this digital wallet is where you can store your ethereum if you get compensated for your work and then convert it back to hard currency (such as USD, Euro, or Pounds) whenever you need it.

- After you've set up your wallet, go to any open marketplace that provides free service in your areas, such as Binance, Gemini, or Kraken, and buy some ethereum there.

- Once you've completed your setup and purchased some ether, simply move it back to your wallet, and you're done. You're now able to get your music distributed across the chain!

- From here, you can go to one of the more common sites, such as Opensea or KnownOrigin where you can sell your art and set the terms and conditions, price, excellent content, and all of that.

- Set up your account on these sites according to the guidelines and create your first NFT.

Why it Matter

The music industry requires a better and stronger future economy, and decentralised NFTs are the answer. While streaming platforms and artist support services have made a big difference in spreading artists' work around the globe and providing avenues for fans worldwide to support their favorite artists, these services often struggle to provide an acceptable return on investment for the art itself.

To make a better environment for our future ravers, shower singers, subway riders, and fans worldwide, we should strive to promote and encourage quality work. NFTs contribute to coming up with a solution to this current problem. They can readjust the value return gap by prioritizing quality of work over the illusion of who an individual is via social networks or streaming algorithms.

Chapter 16:
EXTRAS FOR YOU

Opportunity

The world collectibles market is worth nearly $400 billion today. Collectors' homes and museums are filled with classic vehicles, comic books, fine wines, and even movie props. When the cumulative value of all artwork ever created is factored in, the number is likely to exceed $1 trillion. Rembrandt, a 17th-century painter, produced over 600 paintings during his life, each of which sold for eight figures on average.

Great Assets to Drive Retail Growth

Today, we are on the brink of a paradigm shift. The NFT market implies you can now benefit from previously untradeable products, tickets, antiques, music, and even your Twitter tweets could be sold to a ready audience. Even the conventional world of physical art and collectibles could be affected by the NFT revolution.

- **Impending Benefit**

It might appear strange to acquire the "authentic" copy of something you can conveniently screenshot from your desktop, but the emotional significance of collecting, particularly when it comes to original art, is easy to overlook. Owning an actual item made by a favorite artist, as well as the boasting rights that go with it, are both appealing. This is basically the same as having an original Andy Warhol painting that can be framed, sold, or shared—the only difference is that it's virtual. Plus, since the creators can configure these products to pay them royalties every time the collectible is sold, NFTs finally solve the issue of artists not being paid.

Risk of the NFT market

Despite the increased interest and price, NFTs are not a sure bet. In reality, they seem to be more of a speculative uproar. The comparison to sports cards fits once again, but they may also be compared to other speculative products like sneakers, handbags, or art. They don't generate any cash flow, and conservative investors like Warren Buffett aren't interested in them.

Typically, you can view or virtually download a video clip for free on the web. However, collectors pay a lot of cash to buy the "approved" edition of the clip or art. An expert suggests that there's a lot of space for confusion and price manipulation here. You don't get any royalties from NFTs, and there's no way of knowing how many of one kind are out there.

Since NFTs do not generate cash flow, the only way to profit is for someone else to come along and offer more for them, a tactic known as the "greater fool" tactic of investing. It is dangerous for anyone looking to purchase high-priced collectibles. Presently, the markets are being driven by a lot of more significant fool theory speculation. If you are interested in them, I suggest you don't go out and buy them.

Liquidity risk affects NFTs as well: if no one wishes to purchase your NFT, you probably wouldn't be able to resell it anytime soon, if at all. This is in stark contrast to the stock market, which has readily available liquidity. Some people also address counterparty danger, such as the possibility that the NFT's original creator did not own the sports clip's rights, for instance. Despite this, some traders are turning to NFTs as a means of making fast money. Those who enter and leave at the wrong times normally lose money in this type of business.

It will be beneficial for speculators to exercise extreme caution here and, as with any risky investment, only invest whatever you can afford to lose. It will have its highs and lows, just like every other investment market. There is very little danger in owning an NFT as it will be yours indefinitely or for as long as you want to hold it. However, It's a different story if you're buying NFTs to speculate.

NFTs, on the other hand, are relatively safe in other respects, even though they aren't a good investment. NFTs have a benefit over physical art. While an artwork could be looted from a gallery in a heist, stealing an NFT involves cracking a person user's private key, which is no small job if they've protected it offline as most individuals do or ought to.

NFTs have the following benefits of a blockchain platform: they can be distributed immediately and legitimately, and your ownership is open and free, and autonomous of the network. The technology's most vital asset is also one of its main limitations, an emerging-market research firm that published a study on NFTs in February. Anyone can make an NFT out of practically everything on the net, which implies a variety of "extremely bad" tokens out there. To say what's worth gathering or investing in, you'll need a trained eye.

That holds true for the physical art market, which is typically a haven for the well-informed. It's the same with NFT art. And, while certain people see the NFT market maturing and expanding into the mainstream in the future, they also see a range of additional challenges and uncertainties that new collectors should be aware of. The NFT market has a lot of luck, partially because there aren't any systems in effect to enable individuals to price assets yet. The value of some of the most common types of NFTs increased by around 2,000 percent by 2020. Some excerpts that initially sold for a few dollars on Top Shot are now worth tens of thousands of dollars.

When it comes to liquidity or the ease with which a commodity can be converted into currency, NFTs are much like baseball cards or paintings than bitcoin or stocks since every seller must find a buyer ready to pay a specific price for a unique object. This can place collectors in a challenging situation if, for example, they spent $100,000 on a Top Shot moment and the market collapses.

However, a crypto investor that launched an NFT investment fund in September 2019 told Insider, illiquidity could be a positive thing because it stops individuals from making impulsive decisions. He believes that if individuals don't have the option to panic and sell their NFTs, the market would prevent the kind of valuation declines that would cause such a selloff in the first place.

Ownership of NFTs

Most newcomers to NFTs are unaware that there is usually a difference between the token itself, a blockchain-based record of ownership, and the product it corresponds to, which is typically a picture, video, or audio file kept separately. Buyers may be stuck with tokens pointing to files that no more exist if a firm that released NFTs goes out of business and ceases to host such digital artworks, basketball trading cards, or other media.

There are solutions to this issue and would become the standard in the near future, such as file storage via decentralized services. However, the risk remains. The hairy essence of NFT possession proves that the tokens have no inherent value and that the hype around them is ludicrous. The ownership records themselves are the electronic representation of Beanie Babies: sweet little nothings of no worth beyond what anyone else would buy them.

The Possibility of Fraud and Foul Play

It's difficult to fake an NFT, and it's simple to find out where one originated from. However, that doesn't imply the industry is without shady dealings. Anybody can make an NFT out of a file that isn't owned by them and sell it to naive buyers as their own.

Manipulation similar to that seen in other markets could also be taking place. Wash trading occurs when someone falsely inflates a product's price by opening several accounts and buying and selling with themselves, which has been popular in NFTs in the past. It's a habit that seasoned collectors can spot quickly, but beginners can find it challenging to spot. Since blockchain exchanges are private and permanent, if anyone gains access to your computer and steals your money, you're pretty much screwed.

CONCLUSION

As described in the book's chapters, fungibility refers to the ability to swap one bitcoin for another bitcoin or some other token; for instance, one Golem-ERC20 token is equivalent to another Golem token. The same can be said for OmiseGO tokens, which are fungible. N on-Fungibles, on the other hand, cannot have the same value. The most precise illustration is CryptoKitty, a blockchain-based game that enables you to buy, collect, and digital breed cats; each CryptoKitty is special. Even though you can swap one Kitty for another if both sides consent, they are not made equal otherwise.

This distinction between fungible and non-fungible tokens is necessary to help us understand non-fungible tokens. The knowledge of what NFTs are will help you figure out how they fit into the crypto universe.

Summary of NFT Applications

Gaming

As you are aware, many games require you to spend tokens explicitly created for that game in order to advance to the next level or upgrade your equipment. NFTs are perfect for games where essential objects can be quickly moved, eliminating one of the gamers' greatest annoyances.

Collectibles

The clearest example of collectibles is CryptoKitty'e. NFTs may also be used to create typical collectors' pieces like baseball cards, coins, and stamps.

Art

With difficulty in digital artists securing their copyright, with the aid of NFTs and blockchain-based proof of ownership, it is simple to determine who is using copyrighted content. Also, by eliminating the need for third-party fees and allowing peer-to-peer payments, artists may earn a larger share of their work revenue. This contributes more reason why NFTs are hinted to be the next big thing.

Sports

Counterfeit tickets and merchandise severely harm sports income. Using NFTs to mitigate losses is the best choice.

Identity

Maintaining legal records such as educational certificates, medical histories, and any goods assets records is difficult, but NFTs could digitize all of this and allow data owners more power.

Real Assets

Real-world assets such as real estate are currently being tokenized on the blockchain, although it is possible to tokenize real-world assets using NFTs to show who owns a piece of property.

To Create NFTs, There Must Be Standards

As you are aware, a blockchain platform is required to create any token. Below is a recap of blockchain platforms that support the development of NFTs using various standards.

ERC-721

In its ERC-721 standard, Ethereum became the first blockchain to enable the development of NFTs. ERC-721 tokens, like many other ERC specifications, are powered by smart contract code that embeds the special characteristics that make them uncommon or desirable. This metadata may be kept on or off the blockchain.

ERC-1155

The ERC-1155 was created as a successor to the ERC-721. ERC-1155 is unique in that it enables both fungible and non-fungible products to be included in the same smart contract. In addition, any combination of fungible tokens can be used in a single executed contract in this standard. NFTs can also be generated using the ERC-994, ERC-420, ERC-809, ERC-1201, and ERC-998 specifications.

Summary on NFTs Marketplaces

NFT exchange marketplaces are critical to the spread of NFT boundaries. From the chapters of the book, I've presented a summary of sites where you can index, sell, and pass NFTs.

OpenSea

OpenSea is a well-known NFT marketplace. revisit the chapter on marketplaces to understand the nature of the market

Rarible

Rarible-Website is a website dedicated to rare items. Rarible, like OpenSea, allows you to list and buy NFTs.

SuperRare

As the name implies, this marketplace only sells exclusive and one-of-a-kind digital artworks. It has a more user-friendly interface, social profiles, a mobile app, live auctions, more payment options, and better management.

Enjin Marketplace

The Enjiin marketplace is devoted solely to enjin-based NFTs. It has a web-based interface as well as a native Enjin wallet that allows you to find, purchase, and sell NFTs.

Decentraland

Probably the most popular NFTs marketplace for land. Decentaland is not a marketplace for buying and selling NFTs. Instead, it's a fully decentralized digital world, similar to virtual reality.

Pros and cons of NFTs

NFT has the potential to be a new source of revenue for gaming, sports, art, and technology. NFTs, like Decentaland, have the potential to change our attitudes toward ownership by allowing us to own a real-world product thousands of miles away. Via NFTs, several crypto unknowns will be able to implement cryptocurrencies for the first time. Since nonfungible tokens are still new, designing DApps for them can be difficult and time-consuming.

NFT games would likely have a "hot potato" effect. Players purchase an asset in the hopes of reselling it for a profit, but they risk losing money if the market crashes. Understanding the NFT requires much more simplification, particularly for those who are unfamiliar with blockchain. NFT is still a new technology that needs more exposure.

Wrap UP

NFT is still a new technology that needs more exposure. It appears that major corporations such as IBM, Ubisoft,

Vodafone, Nike, and Samsung are investigating NFT use cases, potentially boosting NFT acceptance.

Public awareness and willingness to try the technology are growing. Brendan Dawes, a UK graphic designer, and artist who uses machine learning and algorithms to create digital art, claims that a piece of one of his works will typically sell for $2,000, but his most recent NFT sold for $37,000.

However, the possibilities don't end there. NFTs can be configured to pay a cryptocurrency fee to their artists and owners every time they change hands. If a buyer of one of Dawes' arts resells it, Dawes receives 10% of the initial sales price. "Again, as opposed to the traditional world, that's one of the possibilities. You'll get a royalty for the rest of your life." This, along with other immense opportunities, is the reason there has been growing acceptance of NFTs.

NFTs are bound to generate excesses since they are crypto. The purchase of a virtual racing car for $100,000 is the peak of some of the prices offered. Some websites offer cryptocurrency loans in return for NFT collaterals with all the makings of a mini-crash waiting to happen. You can imagine the door of endless opportunity that could open in the nearest future should the current acceptance rate continues.

Printed in Great Britain
by Amazon